CHICKEN DINNERS

CHICKEN DINNERS

Twenty-Four Seasonal Menus
Featuring
Delicious, Easy-to-Make Chicken Recipes
for Family Suppers, Dinner Parties and Holidays

LORRAINE BODGER

ILLUSTRATED BY LORRAINE BODGER

HARMONY BOOKS/NEW YORK

Published by Harmony Books, a division of Crown Publishers, Inc., 201 East 50th Street, New York, New York, 10022. Member of the Crown Publishing Group.

HARMONY and colophon are trademarks of Crown Publishers, Inc.

Manufactured in the United States of America

Library of Congress Cataloging-in-Publication Data
Bodger, Lorraine.
    Chicken dinners/Lorraine Bodger.—1st ed.
      p. cm.
    Includes index.
    1. Cookery (Chicken) 2. Entrées (Cookery) 3. Menus. I. Title.
TX750.5.C45B63   1991
641.6′65—dc20   90-25080
                                                          CIP

ISBN 0-517-58540-5

10 9 8 7 6 5 4 3 2 1

First Edition   Designed by Lorraine Bodger

ACKNOWLEDGMENTS

Special thanks to editors Kathy Belden and Peter Guzzardi for their care and support, to Delia Ephron and Jerry Kass for their hospitality and the use of their new kitchen, to David Glaser for advice about chicken broth, to Jane Weiss for menu consultation and to all the other dear friends and relations who helped Lowell and me eat a considerable number of chicken dinners.

CONTENTS

FOREWORD

Lorrie, which is what her friends call Lorraine Bodger, arrived at our home in January for a working vacation. She was testing recipes for CHICKEN DINNERS and her effect on our household was a little like the effect Mary Poppins had when she arrived at the Banks home.

My teenage stepdaughter and her friends would come from school. "Oh, it smells so good here," they would say, and instead of heading for Julie's bedroom and privacy, they would all bounce into the kitchen and sit down, sampling and gabbing. I heard more about Julie's life in those two weeks than I had in six months. All credit due to the socializing influence of stir-fried chicken on crisp noodles and mocha custard—just to name two of Julie's "absolute favorites." During Lorrie's visit, I also saw Julie consume food that she would not normally touch. "Mmm," she would say, popping in a bit of mango tart, savoring some poached pear in wine sauce or wild rice with pecans, nibbling at Lorrie's fabulous batter-fried chicken.

My husband, a writer, works at home. Every day around one, Lorrie would knock on his office door to say that lunch was ready, and they would sample her morning recipes. "I feel like I'm living in someone's country estate," he would say when he phoned with the mouth-watering details.

Then I would come home and dinner was prepared. Sometimes with not one main course but two or three, depending on how many recipes Lorrie had tested. The first time I went into mild shock: You mean I just get to eat, I don't have to cook? But I quickly recovered in time to devour a sinful amount of Lorrie's Chicken Milanaise and grilled vegetables—endive, radicchio, mushrooms, onions, eggplant all faintly drizzled with a lovely garlic-flavored oil.

It's true that, for the weeks Lorrie was with us, we did eat a lot of chicken, but that's all we ever eat anyway—chicken and pasta. (And Lorrie just happened to be testing a great pasta for this book—a cold pasta salad with olives and yellow peppers.) Besides, Lorrie understands exactly how we like our food—irresistible, healthy, satisfying but not fussy. She knows that we love a decadent dessert but that basically, when we get up from the table, we want to be able to move easily from one room to the next and not have to lie about for an hour with moans and regrets.

We still talk about Lorrie's visit—the two weeks in which the food on the table made life so much more delicious. Of course, everyone can't be as lucky as we were, but they can have this book. It's the next best thing to having Lorrie in your life.

Delia Ephron

INTRODUCTION

If you're eating like a lot of American families, you're eating more chicken. I don't have to tell you how versatile chicken is; that it's great hot, cold or in between; how well it goes with rice, pasta, beans, potatoes or any other kind of starch; how it complements almost every kind of vegetable and a few fruits, too; what a great soup or sandwich it makes; how it works for every occasion from the simplest lunch to the fanciest dinner; how appropriate it is in every season. You know all this.

In fact, you probably have a handful of chicken recipes that you repeat fairly regularly for the family, and one or two you dust off for company. Now, when chicken is such an important element of the way we eat, it's time to stop juggling the same old recipes and get going on some all-new chicken dinners.

In this book you'll find 24 chicken dinner menus—weekday dinners, make-ahead meals (high on my list of favorites), interesting menus for guests, comforting winter suppers, leisurely summer grills. Each menu includes all the recipes you'll need, plus extra Notes on the Menus to help you vary the dinners, to make them simpler or jazzier.

And for heaven's sake, don't hesitate to use the chicken recipes in combination with your own favorite side dishes and desserts. Or to pick an appetizer recipe from one menu, a chicken recipe from another and a dessert from a third. Mix and match is the name of the game if you want even more flexibility than the book already gives you. Follow the menus you love, rely on them when you don't have time to plan (or you're a bit nervous about inventing your own), but feel free to adapt them to your needs and preferences.

Finally, don't miss the helpful hints and suggestions that run across the bottom of many of the pages of *Chicken Dinners*. Look for special menus for special occasions (like Easter dinner or a wedding luncheon), tips on entertaining, pretty table settings, simple garnishes, holiday centerpieces and a great deal more.

CHAPTER 1
CHICKEN BASICS

This chapter includes everything you need to know in order to use and enjoy the menus and recipes in this book. Chicken Basics is not The Complete Guide to Chicken, but it is full of important information and I hope you will read it and refer to it when you have a question.

WHICH CHICKEN IS BEST?

For all the debates about which brand of chicken has the best flavor and texture and which kind (free-range, supermarket, organic, kosher or premium) is superior, I have found that the kind of chicken you buy on a regular basis is generally dictated by what is easily accessible and what you can afford. As simple as that. If you're near a butcher and you can afford the extra cash per pound, you'll probably buy the premium or kosher brands. If you make one weekly trip to a supermarket, you'll buy whatever chicken is fresh (and perhaps on sale) that day and not give it another thought.

I've also found that most cooks have strong prejudices: Whatever chicken they're accustomed to cooking is the one that tastes best—and no one can convince them otherwise.

So let's be realistic here. I'll tell you what I generally prefer and you'll either try it or you won't: I prefer premium-brand chickens to supermarket brands, not because the flavor is necessarily superior but because I think the texture is significantly better. I also prefer my favorite premium brand of chicken over kosher chickens, which are sometimes a bit salty for my taste.

More realism: It's pointless for a cookbook to recommend a specific brand of chicken since different brands are available in different parts of the country. If you're interested in finding a better chicken in your area, ask a few good cooks which brands they like. Try them and decide for yourself.

MY KIND OF CHICKEN

Chickens come in a lot of sizes, from the smallest Rock Cornish hen to the biggest eight-pound roaster. The chicken that seems to be most useful and most available is between three and four pounds and is usually called a broiler/fryer. It ought to be called a roaster/fryer, since you're more likely to roast it (or cook its parts by some other oven method) than broil it. However, I suppose the poultry industry doesn't want you to confuse it with the four- to eight-pounders that are called roasters.

I like the all-purpose three- to four-pound chicken. The recipes in this book are based on that bird, whole and cut in parts.

HOW MUCH CHICKEN?

This is a tough question to answer for the obvious reason: appetites vary. One answer is that the amount of chicken called for in each recipe is meant to serve six ordinary adult diners. You'll notice, too, that the amount of chicken in the recipes varies somewhat according to the type of dish and the menu in which it is found.

A more general answer is that a 3½-pound whole chicken is considered enough to serve three or four people, so for six people, prepare two whole chickens. When chicken parts are required, serve at least two per person and sometimes more if the parts are small or the appetites are large.

CHICKEN PARTS

It's helpful to define our terms here, so you can buy or cut for yourself the parts needed for each recipe.

A whole chicken may be cut into halves:

← cut through breast and then backbone

Or quarters (a breast quarter being half of the breast plus one wing, and part of the back; a leg quarter being one drumstick plus one thigh, and part of the back):

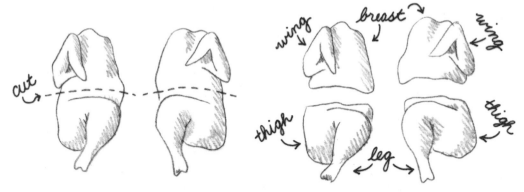

Or parts:

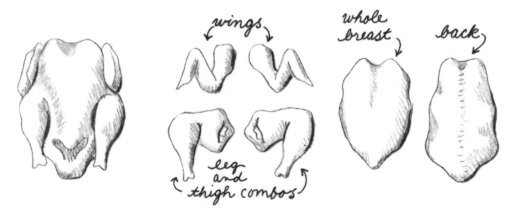

Certain parts may be cut into even smaller portions:

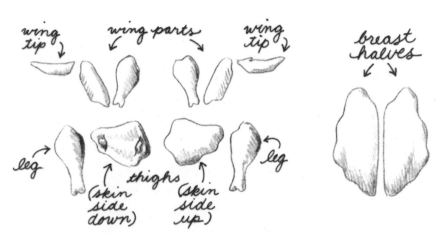

When you ask your butcher to cut a whole chicken "in eight," he will cut it into eight serving pieces: two wings, two thighs, two drumsticks, two breast halves. The back is a separate piece, not usually regarded as suitable for serving since it has very little meat on it. However, it is excellent for making broth or soup, so be sure the butcher puts it in your package.

In addition to the parts shown in the drawings, you will on occasion want to buy whole boneless chicken breasts. Although they are more expensive, boneless breasts are great time-savers since all the tedious work of boning has been done for you. Most recipes that list whole boneless breasts in the ingredients will require you to pull off the skin and then cut the whole breasts in half.

HEALTH AND SAFETY

Before we go any further, to the point of actually handling the chicken, let's take care of important business: Chicken is extremely perishable, so when you're preparing and cooking it (and many other foods, too), you must take sensible precautions to avoid or kill bacteria that may produce food poisoning.

1. Refrigerate raw chicken as soon as possible. Make sure the chicken is contained in such a way that it does not touch or drip on other foods in the refrigerator.

2. Wash your hands before and after handling chicken.

3. Rinse raw chicken in cold water, but don't let the rinse water get on any dishes in the sink or on any other foods. Wash hands, colander and sink well.

4. Any surfaces, countertops, utensils, cutting boards, knives, appliances, sponges, etc., touched by raw chicken (or the juice from raw chicken) should be washed thoroughly with warm water and soap before being used again; this prevents cross-contamination. Have a separate, nonporous cutting board to use with chicken and keep it clean.

5. Defrost chicken in the refrigerator, never at room temperature.

6. Cook raw chicken within one or two days of buying it. Smell the chicken before handling it; if it smells bad, discard it or, better still, return it to the place of purchase—and complain to the manager. However, many bacteria are completely odorless, so you must observe safety precautions even with fresh-smelling chicken.

7. Cook chicken thoroughly (more on this subject on pages 7–8).

8. Refrigerate cooked chicken as soon as possible; do not leave it at room temperature for more than a couple of hours. Be especially careful in hot summer weather.

9. Never put cooked chicken back in a container or on a platter that previously held raw chicken (unless you first wash the container carefully, of course).

10. Refrigerate or freeze leftovers as soon as possible.

PREPARING RAW CHICKEN

These basic preparations are not mentioned in any recipe because it is assumed that either you know them already or that after reading them here, you will do them routinely before following the recipe.

Whole chicken

Remove the loose or packaged giblets and neck from the cavity. Rinse the chicken inside and out and pat dry with paper towels. Pull off any large chunks of fat around the openings. If needed, cut the chicken into the parts required in the recipe.

Chicken parts

Rinse the parts and pat them dry with paper towels. Depending on the recipe, you may then cut them into smaller parts (pages 2–4). Discard any cartilage, chips of bone or other unwanted bits, including fat. If the recipe requires skinless chicken parts (especially chicken breasts), simply pull off the skin, using a small sharp knife to help.

Note: Breasts and thighs are easy to skin; drumsticks are a little trickier (slit the skin lengthwise, peel it down and cut it away around the ankle) and wings are virtually impossible.

CUTTING UP RAW CHICKEN

When raw chicken parts are needed for a recipe, whole raw chickens must, of course, be cut up to provide them. Most cutting up involves standard techniques: cutting a whole chicken into eight serving pieces; cutting the whole chicken leg into thigh and drumstick; cutting a whole breast in half; boning a breast or thigh. Either do these things yourself, have the butcher do them for you or buy chicken that is already cut up or boned.

ADDITIONAL TECHNIQUES

Trussing

Many people feel it is important to truss a raw whole chicken (to tuck the wings under and tie the legs together to make a neater and more compact shape) before roasting it, claiming that trussing yields a juicier bird. I have found that it just isn't so. Trussing is strictly an esthetic measure, because it prevents the chicken legs from splaying during roasting. If I'm planning to bring the whole roasted chicken to the table, I simply cross the ankles and tie them together before roasting so the chicken looks pretty when cooked; if I'm planning to carve in the kitchen, I don't bother trussing at all.

Marinating

Marination is a way of preparing raw chicken parts for cooking, *after* you have carried out the basic steps above. Marinating means steeping the chicken (or other food) in a seasoned liquid (marinade) until the flavor of the marinade is absorbed.

Marinating a chicken can't be accomplished in twenty minutes or one hour; it takes time, at least several hours or even overnight. And since it takes time, the chicken must be refrigerated while it marinates.

Pounding

Boneless, skinless raw chicken breasts are often pounded flat to make cutlets of an even thickness. These cutlets are rather elegant and a great convenience as well, since they cook quickly and take on a lot of flavor from any wine, sauce or seasoning that is cooked with them.

You can use a mallet, rolling pin or some other smooth heavy object, but my favorite pounding tool is designed specifically for the job. The nonslip handle is grooved for a firm grip and the metal disk is weighted for quick results without strain.

Lay the chicken breast on a firm board or counter, with the rougher side up (the shiny, smooth side is not as pliable). Hit hard with the flat surface of the pounder, pushing the flesh outward. To flatten the thicker sections easily, whack them lightly with the edge of the pounder to break down the fibers, then resume pounding.

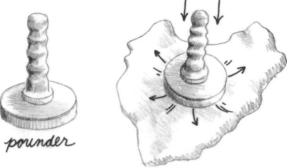

pounder

COOKING THE CHICKEN

Whatever the method—baking, roasting, poaching, etc.—it is important that chicken be thoroughly cooked. How can you tell if the chicken is cooked enough? One way is to check the internal temperature with an instant-reading thermometer, inserting the thermometer in the breast meat and/or the thickest part of the thigh, taking care not to touch any bone. Although the USDA recommends cooking poultry to a minimum internal temperature of 160°, more conservative sources suggest that temperatures should read at least 170° at the breast and 185°–190° at the thigh.

For a whole chicken, you can also use the time-honored tests of doneness— wiggling the drumstick to see if it moves easily, pinching the thigh to feel if it is soft, puncturing the skin near the thigh to see if the juices that run out are clear or cutting into the flesh to see if it has completely lost its pinkness.

But these methods aren't convenient for all recipes: You can't pinch a thigh that's covered with sauce and vegetables. However, you may rely on the recipes in this book to give you correct cooking times—and you should rely on your own experience as well.

A word about your oven

When you set your oven thermostat, the oven should heat to the correct temperature. This is important for all recipes (and especially for baking), so buy a mercury-type oven thermometer and use it whenever you turn on the oven: Place the thermometer in the center of the oven, turn on the heat and wait

15 minutes. Adjust the thermostat according to the thermometer reading. Leave the oven open for a minute, close the door, wait ten more minutes and check again.

After you've done this checking procedure a few times, you'll know how to set your oven to compensate for any glitches in the thermostat. However, if your oven is consistently off by more than 25 degrees, it's a good idea to have it corrected by a professional.

Notes on cooking techniques

Browning: I often think browning should be called "goldening" instead. It can take quite some time to get chicken parts really brown, even light brown, so I generally settle for golden. You'll notice that it's hardest to brown the first batch of chicken pieces in the skillet; the second batch is easier because the skillet now has lots of little brown bits stuck to it, and the bits lend color to the sautéed chicken.

Roasting and baking: These are confusing terms since they mean just about the same thing—cooking in dry oven heat. The only difference is that foods are not covered during roasting but they may be covered during baking.

Sautéing, poaching and braising: Sautéing is cooking in a small amount of oil, butter or margarine in a skillet over direct heat. Poaching is cooking in simmering liquid, usually over direct heat. Braising is a combination of both—sautéing first, then adding liquid, covering the pan and simmering until tender.

Oven-frying: This is not frying at all. Oven-frying means coating the chicken with crumbs and baking it in the oven to simulate—without oil—the crisp quality of deep-fried food.

INGREDIENTS

Certain items appear regularly in the ingredients lists preceding each set of recipe steps, and the following will provide helpful information about these basics.

Chicken broth and chicken stock

For the recipes in this book, it is *not* necessary to make your own stock or broth. (However, if you want to prepare your own broth, turn to page 11.) In this book, not only are stock and broth interchangeable, but homemade and store-bought are, too. This ingredient is always listed simply as "chicken broth."

Please remember that canned broths vary widely in saltiness, intensity of chicken flavor, ingredients, size of can and price. As with brands of chicken, brands of broth command intense loyalty—you're probably convinced that your favorite brand is the best. I do suggest that you try a different one occasionally; tastes change and you may find one you like better.

Although I tested the chicken recipes using several different brands of broth, I can't guarantee that every recipe will taste the same regardless of the brand used. Be prepared to add seasoning or dilute the broth, if you feel it is necessary.

Notes on a few other ingredients

There are staples (aside from chicken broth) that should be mentioned because they always mean the same thing throughout the ingredients lists.

Butter: This means sweet, unsalted butter. If you must use salted butter, reduce the amount of salt called for in the recipe.

Eggs: Use large ones.

Flour: Use all-purpose unless otherwise indicated.

Sugar: Use white granulated unless otherwise indicated.

Fresh pepper: Grind peppercorns in a pepper grinder.

If it is especially important to use a particular ingredient, it is described in the ingredients list. For instance, if you see **light brown sugar** listed, that's what you should use—not dark brown. On the other hand, if **brown sugar** is listed, you may use either light or dark brown sugar.

When a distinctively flavored oil (such as olive, peanut or sesame oil) is essential to the recipe, it is listed by name in the ingredients. When vegetable oil is listed, choose a mild-flavored favorite—safflower, corn, sunflower, etc.

Dried herbs (as opposed to fresh ones) must sometimes be powdered or crumbled before use. To powder them, crush the flakes of dried herb either by rubbing them between your fingertips or the palms of your hands until pulverised. To crumble, simply rub until the flakes are smaller but not powdered.

Preparing fresh produce

Before use, vegetables, fruits and other fresh produce must be washed and usually patted dry on paper towels or shaken as dry as possible in a colander (or salad spinner, for leafy vegetables). The recipes often call for trimming the vegetables, too, which means cutting off one or both ends as shown in the drawings. After trimming, some vegetables are peeled with a vegetable peeler.

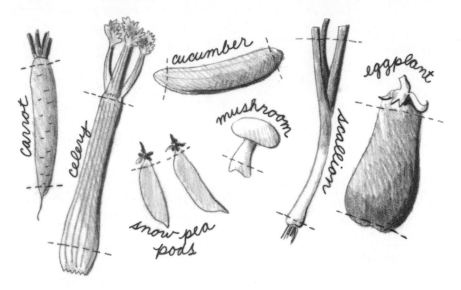

The following specific instructions apply throughout the recipes.

Cabbage (green, red or Chinese): Trim or cut out stem end; discard wilted or yellowed outer leaves.

Carrots: Trim tops and tails; peel.

Celery: Trim stem and opposite end, removing little branches with leaves (unless the leaves are needed in the recipe).

Cucumber: Trim at least half an inch of each end; peel waxy or thick skin (not necessary with Kirby cucumbers); if required, slit lengthwise and use a spoon to scoop out the seeds.

Eggplant: Trim stem end and a quarter-inch of opposite end.

Garlic, shallots, onions: Cut off both ends; peel off papery skin.

Ginger: Using a small, sharp knife, peel only as much as you need.

Lettuce: Discard wilted or yellow outer leaves; cut out stem end; separate leaves and wash well to remove dirt and sand; spin or pat leaves completely dry.

Mushrooms: Trim stem ends; wipe caps clean with damp paper towel.

Parsley, coriander, basil: Use only the leaves; discard stems.

Scallions: Cut off root ends; trim withered greens.

Snow pea pods: Trim stem ends.

Spinach and other dark greens: Remove thick stems; wash well to remove dirt and sand.

Sweet or hot pepper: If pepper is to be roasted, follow instructions on page 54. Raw or roasted, cut out and discard stem end and attached seeds; cut in half; rinse out the remaining seeds; devein by paring away the white membranes (veins) inside.

BASIC RECIPE:
RICH CHICKEN BROTH

Makes 8 cups

This is perfect for use whenever chicken broth is required in the recipes. You'll need a 10- or 12-quart pot or kettle to make it.

Note: Since you'll have to shop for backs, necks and other parts of chicken, you might like to buy a whole chicken, too, and poach it to perfection in your pot of beautiful homemade stock. (See Basic Recipe: Whole Chicken Poached in Broth, page 12.)

8 pounds chicken bones, wing tips, wings, backs, necks and giblets (except livers)
1 large onion, quartered
2 large carrots, trimmed, peeled and cut in half

3 stalks celery with leaves, trimmed and cut in thirds
2 teaspoons salt
18–20 whole peppercorns
Generous handful flat-leaf (Italian) parsley leaves
16 cups (4 quarts) water

1. Remove as much fat as possible from the chicken backs. Rinse all the chicken parts and put them in a 10- or 12-quart kettle or stockpot. Add the remaining ingredients and the water (which should cover the chicken).

With the pot covered, bring to a boil over high heat. Lower the heat immediately, remove the lid and simmer for 2 hours, skimming occasionally to remove foam.

2. With a slotted spoon, lift out and discard the chicken parts and vegetables. Pour the broth through a fine strainer into another deep kettle or stockpot. Simmer uncovered for 1 more hour to reduce the broth to about 8 cups. Taste and add more salt if necessary.

3. Cover and refrigerate the broth until the fat hardens on the surface. Remove the fat and use the broth for any recipe requiring chicken broth or freeze it for future use.

BASIC RECIPE:
WHOLE CHICKEN
POACHED IN BROTH

Makes 3½–4 cups of cooked chicken

Even though no recipe in this book calls specifically for a whole poached chicken, try the basic recipe anyway—the cooked chicken it yields is moist and flavorful, perfect for chicken salads and sandwiches.

1 whole chicken, 3½–4 pounds
8 cups Rich Chicken Broth (page 11) or canned chicken broth

2 carrots, peeled, trimmed and cut in half
1 parsnip, peeled and trimmed

1. Rinse the chicken and remove the excess fat from the entrance to the cavity. Put the chicken in a pot filled with the broth (the chicken should be mostly submerged), cover tightly and bring to a boil. Reduce the heat, tilt the lid a bit so a little steam can escape and simmer for 30 minutes.

2. Add the carrots and parsnip and simmer until the vegetables are tender, about 20 more minutes. Carefully remove the chicken (it will be falling off the bone) and set aside to cool. Discard the parsnip, but save the carrots, if you like, for adding to soup.

3. Pour the broth by the cupful through a fine strainer into a deep bowl, noting how many cups you have. Add enough water to make 8 cups.

Cover and refrigerate until the fat hardens on the surface; remove the fat. Use the rich soup for any recipe requiring chicken broth, or freeze for future use.

BASIC RECIPE:
PERFECT POACHED CHICKEN BREASTS

Makes 2½–3 cups cooked chicken

Several of the recipes in this book call for poached chicken breasts. They're so easy to make that you may want to double the poaching recipe and freeze half the chicken for another time.

3 whole chicken breasts (with bones), halved

1 tablespoon butter
½ cup chicken broth

1. Have ready 1 large skillet (12–14 inches in diameter) or 2 smaller ones. Pull off and discard as much skin and fat as you can from the chicken breasts. Rinse them well.

2. Put the butter and broth in the large skillet (or half of each in each smaller skillet) and bring to a simmer. Place the chicken, flesh side up, in the skillet (or half the chicken in each smaller skillet). Cover the skillet, tilting the lid slightly so a little steam can escape during cooking.

3. Cook the chicken for 15 minutes, keeping the broth at a simmer (not a boil) over low heat. Then turn off the heat and leave the chicken in the skillet for 15 more minutes.

Cut into 1 piece of chicken (or 1 piece in each skillet) to see if the meat is cooked through. If the meat is pink, turn the heat back on and simmer for 5 more minutes.

4. Lift the chicken from the hot broth and rinse in cold water; refrigerate until cool. Separate the chicken meat from the bones, discarding the bones as well as any bits of fat and gristle. Refrigerate the chicken until needed; strain the broth into a container and refrigerate or freeze for future use.

CHAPTER 2
CHICKEN DINNERS FOR SPRING

Menu #1
OVEN-FRIED CHICKEN WINGS WITH CHILI BARBECUE SAUCE

Menu #2
COLD CHICKEN AND SPICY SESAME NOODLES

Menu #3
SCALLION PANCAKES WITH SAVORY CHICKEN FILLING

Menu #4
PAELLA

Menu #5
ROASTED CHICKEN WITH HERB AND GARLIC BUTTER

Menu #6
MARINATED, BAKED ASIAN CHICKEN

Chicken dinners for spring reflect the changing season. Appetites are still hearty, since the weather is pleasantly cool, but robust winter menus no longer feel quite suitable. Spring menus begin to lighten up, featuring chicken served with fresh new green vegetables (asparagus, baby artichokes, peas) and piquant sauces, followed by light desserts of strawberries, cherries, mangoes or pineapple, crisp cookies and tender cake.

This is a good place to emphasize that any chicken dish can be appropriate to any season, depending on what you serve with it. The chicken recipes in this book are, in fact, delicious in every season, when mixed and matched with appropriate appetizers, vegetables and desserts. The menus are here for you to use either as they stand or as starting points for creating your own dinners.

Note: When you read the menus, you'll see that some of the dishes are listed in *italics*. This tells you that they are so simple or standard that no recipes are needed for them. I'm assuming you know how to put together such basics as a bowl of strawberries and cream or a mixed green salad (though you'll find some good ideas for salad on pages 24 and 46).

Spring Menu #1

Mixed green salad with spring radishes
Blue Cheese Dressing

OVEN-FRIED CHICKEN WINGS WITH CHILI BARBECUE SAUCE

Fresh Asparagus with Browned Shallots
Drop Biscuits

Grandmother's Sand Cookies
Strawberries and cream

This is a casual meal eaten mostly with your fingers, so serve it to family or good friends—folks who won't mind if you wind up with Chili Barbecue Sauce on your chin.

NOTES ON THE MENU

Adding a dish of buttered rice spiked with minced fresh parsley or chives stretches the meal for a hungry group.

On the other hand, if you're short on time and want to scale down the menu, skip the Chili Barbecue Sauce altogether and serve the asparagus steamed and dotted with butter (and a squeeze of lemon, if you like). Substitute bakery cookies for the homemade sand cookies.

Spring Produce Buying Guide

Look for and enjoy the following in spring:

Artichokes	Mustard greens	Okra	Spinach	Apricots
Asparagus	New potatoes	Radishes	Sugar snap peas	Cantaloupe
Chard		Scallions		Cherries
Dandelion greens				Mangoes
Green peas				Papayas
Jícama				Rhubarb
Kohlrabi				Strawberries

BLUE CHEESE DRESSING

Makes about 1 cup

My husband's favorite. One of mine, too, since it takes only minutes to make (or make ahead).

¼ **pound blue cheese**
5 **tablespoons mayonnaise**
5 **tablespoons sour cream**
2 **tablespoons water**
2 **tablespoons red or white wine vinegar**
Fresh pepper to taste

Purée half the blue cheese with all the other ingredients, including a generous grinding of fresh pepper. Crumble and add the rest of the blue cheese, stir well and use to dress a mixed green salad.

OVEN-FRIED CHICKEN WINGS WITH CHILI BARBECUE SAUCE

Makes plenty for 6

This is definitely finger food, crisp and crunchy without being greasy, and ready for dipping in piquant barbecue sauce. The Ritz crackers really make this chicken, but no one will guess you used them unless you choose to tell.

Butter or margarine, room temperature, for greasing the pans
24 **chicken wings, wing tips removed**
1½ **cups evaporated milk (one 12-ounce can)**

½ **pound Ritz crackers, crushed to fine crumbs (about 2⅓ cups)**
Note: Crush with a rolling pin or in your food processor.
1 **teaspoon salt**
Fresh pepper
Chili Barbecue Sauce (recipe follows)

1. Preheat the oven to 375°. Line 2 baking sheets or jelly-roll pans with foil; brush foil generously with butter or margarine.

2. Place the chicken wings in a large bowl and pour the evaporated milk over them. Stir to moisten thoroughly.

3. In another bowl or on a large piece of wax paper, mix together the cracker crumbs, salt and a good grinding of fresh pepper. One at a time, dredge the chicken wings in crumbs and transfer to the foil-lined baking sheets, making 1 layer of wings on each sheet.

Bake for 45–55 minutes, or until the chicken is tender. Serve hot or cold with Chili Barbecue Sauce on the side for dipping.

CHILI BARBECUE SAUCE
Makes about 2 cups

1½ cups drained and finely chopped canned Italian-style tomatoes (about one 35-ounce can)
½ cup chopped onion (about 1 small onion)
3 tablespoons tomato paste
¼ cup water
¼ cup cider vinegar
2 tablespoons (packed) brown sugar

2 teaspoons dry mustard
¼ teaspoon hot red pepper flakes
Pinch of celery seed
Salt and pepper to taste

In an uncovered, nonreactive saucepan (stainless steel, enameled, etc.), simmer all the ingredients for 30 minutes, stirring often. Serve warm or cool.

Strawberries

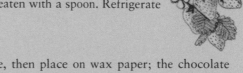

Rinse well and pat dry on paper towels. Hull the berries (remove the stems and leaves) only if they are to be eaten with a spoon. Refrigerate and use within a day or two.

Chocolate-dipped strawberries: Wash berries (with stems and leaves), pat as dry as possible and then allow to air-dry completely. In a small bowl over a saucepan of simmering water, melt 3 ounces of semisweet chocolate with 1 teaspoon vegetable oil, stirring until smooth. Holding each berry by the stem or leaves, dip it halfway into the melted chocolate, then place on wax paper; the chocolate will harden in about 2 hours.

Strawberries and cream: Hull and slice berries or cut in wedge-shaped quarters. Stir berries with a little superfine sugar and serve with a pitcher of heavy cream or with softly whipped, lightly sweetened cream.

FRESH ASPARAGUS
WITH BROWNED SHALLOTS

Makes enough for 6

Asparagus—especially the pencil-thin size that is usually available only in spring—is a treat not to be missed. It's best eaten with your fingers, just like the oven-fried chicken.

2 tablespoons olive oil
1 tablespoon butter
¼ pound shallots, minced

2½ pounds thin asparagus, woody
　stems snapped off
Salt

1. Heat the olive oil and butter in a large skillet. Add the minced shallots and sauté over low heat until very soft and lightly browned. Set the skillet aside.

2. Cook the asparagus by your favorite method. Do not overcook; it should be just crisp-tender. Drain well and place the spears in the large skillet with the shallots.

3. Salt the asparagus lightly and smear the shallot mixture all over the asparagus. Warm thoroughly over low heat without letting the shallots burn.

Fresh Pineapple

Ripe pineapples are firm and heavy and have a definite pineapple aroma. Prepare them for eating in one of two ways:

1. Cut off the top and bottom and pare off the brown skin. Remove the eyes by cutting in a spiral direction, then slice thickly and remove the core from each slice with a biscuit cutter or sharp knife, as shown. Cut in large or small pieces.

DROP BISCUITS

Makes 18 biscuits

These biscuits are a snap to make. They freeze well, too, so if 18 is not enough for your biscuit-loving crowd, double the recipe and freeze any leftovers.

2 cups flour
½ teaspoon salt
2 teaspoons baking powder

6 tablespoons cold margarine, cut
   in pats
1 cup milk

1. Preheat the oven to 425°; grease 2 baking sheets.

Put the flour, salt and baking powder in a food processor and process briefly to combine.

2. Add the margarine and process until the mixture resembles corn meal; do not overprocess. Turn out into a bowl.

3. Add the milk and stir just until all the ingredients are well moistened. The dough will be soft and sticky. Drop heaping tablespoons of dough onto the greased baking sheets, leaving 1 inch between biscuits.

4. Bake for 15 minutes, or until well browned on the bottom and lightly browned on top. Serve immediately or set aside until needed; reheat the biscuits in a low oven before serving.

Note: Frozen biscuits should be thawed and then reheated in a low oven.

2. Cut the entire pineapple in wedge-shaped quarters. Slice out the core. With a sharp knife, separate the flesh from the skin. Cut the flesh crosswise in slices and arrange the slices in the shells as shown.

GRANDMOTHER'S SAND COOKIES

Makes about 5 dozen cookies

This recipe is adapted from a family favorite contributed by Susan Sprott. For Christmas and other major occasions, Susan triples the amount. Make the cookies ahead, if you like, and freeze until needed; bring to room temperature before serving.

1¾ cups flour
½ teaspoon salt
1 teaspoon baking powder
8 tablespoons (1 stick) butter, room
    temperature
¾ cup sugar

2 egg yolks
1 tablespoon milk or cream
½ teaspoon vanilla extract
Grated rind from 1 medium lemon
    (about 1½ teaspoons)

1. In a small bowl, stir together the flour, salt and baking powder. Set aside.

2. In a large bowl, cream the butter and sugar. Add the egg yolks, milk or cream, vanilla and grated lemon rind and beat well.

3. Gradually add the dry ingredients, blending well after each addition. Divide the dough in half, shape each half into a flat round and wrap in plastic. Chill for about 1 hour, just until cool and firm enough to roll.

4. Preheat the oven to 375°; grease 2 baking sheets.

On a lightly floured surface, roll out 1 package of dough to ⅛ inch thick. Cut with your favorite cookie cutters and transfer the cookies to a baking sheet, leaving 1 inch between cookies. Save the excess dough for rerolling.

5. Bake for 9–11 minutes, or until the cookies are pale tan on top and golden on the edges. Let the cookies cool on the baking sheet on a wire rack for 5 minutes, then transfer the cookies to the rack to finish cooling.

While the first sheet is baking, roll and cut another batch of cookies and place them on the second baking sheet. Continue in this manner until the dough is used up or you have as many cookies as you want. Freeze any extra dough for use at another time.

Spring Menu #2

Easy Hot and Sour Soup with Tofu and Asparagus

COLD CHICKEN
AND SPICY SESAME NOODLES

Spinach and Mushrooms in Soy-Butter Sauce

*Vanilla ice cream topped with
almond liqueur and toasted slivered almonds
Cherries*

A great deal can be done ahead of time when you're making this Asian-style dinner, which makes it perfect for company as well as family. Check the recipes for make-ahead advice.

NOTES ON THE MENU

A simple way to extend the meal, if necessary, is to add several more ingredients to the soup—slivers of ham, sliced water chestnuts, snow pea pods, thin-sliced Chinese cabbage. You might also like to serve Cold Spiced Eggplant (page 116) or cold marinated string beans with the meal.

How to Toast Nuts

Spread whole or chopped nuts (including almonds, cashews, walnuts, pecans, hazelnuts and pine nuts) on an ungreased jelly roll pan or other shallow baking pan and place in a preheated 350° oven for five to ten minutes. The nuts are done when they smell toasty and a cooled nut is crunchy. Watch them carefully to avoid burning. Let the nuts cool in the pan on a wire rack.

Note: After toasting hazelnuts, remove the paper skins by rubbing a few nuts at a time between your palms or in a rough dish towel.

EASY HOT AND SOUR SOUP WITH TOFU AND ASPARAGUS

Makes about 5 cups

This is a light, porkless version of the traditionally hearty hot and sour soup. May be made ahead and reheated just before serving.

1 cake (10–12 ounces) fresh firm
    tofu (bean curd), rinsed and
    dried
6 medium stalks of asparagus,
    woody stems broken off
4 cups chicken broth

1 teaspoon sugar
3 tablespoons cider vinegar
1 tablespoon soy sauce
¼ teaspoon fresh pepper
3 dashes Tabasco sauce

1. Cut the tofu into ½-inch squares. Peel the asparagus stems if they are tough or gritty; cut the asparagus in ⅛-inch slices, on a steep diagonal.

2. Put all the ingredients except the asparagus in a large saucepan; cover the pan and bring to a boil. Reduce the heat and simmer, uncovered, for 10 minutes. Add the asparagus and cook for 1 more minute.

Serve hot or refrigerate until needed and then reheat.

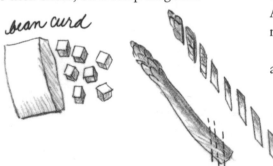

bean curd

Salad Greens, Reds and Whites

For a tossed salad or a bed of greens, the selection of lettuces and other leafy raw vegetables is extensive. Here is a reminder list:

Arugula	Dandelion greens	Mustard greens	Red and green leaf lettuce
Belgian endive	Escarole	Oak-leaf lettuce	Romaine lettuce
Bibb lettuce	Mâche	Radicchio	Savoy cabbage
Boston lettuce		Red cabbage	Spinach
Chicory			Watercress

COLD CHICKEN
AND *SPICY SESAME NOODLES*

Makes plenty for 6

One of my standby main courses, since the chicken and sauce can be prepared quickly or even made a day ahead. All you'll have to do, about an hour before serving, is cook and dress the noodles and assemble the dish.

Note: These noodles are hot and spicy, so if you don't like fiery flavors, cut down or eliminate the red pepper flakes. The sauce will be different but just as tasty.

For the sauce
4½ tablespoons vegetable oil
9 cloves garlic, minced
9 medium scallions, white parts only, minced
   Note: Reserve the green parts for the garnish (see below).
1½ tablespoons peeled, minced ginger
¾ teaspoon hot red pepper flakes
3 tablespoons rice vinegar
3 tablespoons soy sauce
3½ tablespoons sugar
5 tablespoons tahini (sesame paste)
1½ cups chicken or vegetable broth

1 pound linguine or spaghetti (or 1¼ pounds for a really hungry group)

Salt (optional)
2 whole chicken breasts, poached, skinned, boned and cut in bite-size pieces (see page 13 for poaching instructions)
1 large cucumber, trimmed, peeled, seeded and sliced thin
2 teaspoons sesame seeds, toasted, for the garnish
   Note: To toast, place sesame seeds in a small skillet and cook over medium heat, shaking and stirring the seeds, until they turn light brown; watch very carefully to avoid burning.
¼ cup minced scallions, green parts only, for garnish

1. Make the sauce: In a skillet over low heat, heat the oil and sauté the garlic, scallions, ginger and pepper flakes until the garlic is soft but not brown. Turn off the heat.

Add the vinegar, soy sauce, sugar, tahini and 1 cup of the broth. Bring the mixture to a simmer and cook for 5 minutes, stirring constantly and mashing the tahini until it dissolves. Stir in the remaining ½ cup of broth and simmer another minute. Set aside.

2. Cook the linguine or spaghetti in a large pot of salted or unsalted boiling water, just until al dente. Drain in a colander and return the noodles to the pot.

3. Assemble the dish: Pour the sauce over the warm noodles and toss to coat thoroughly. Mound the noodles in the center of a large platter and surround with the chicken pieces. Arrange the cucumber slices as a border around the chicken. Sprinkle the toasted sesame seeds on the noodles and the minced scallions (green parts) on the cucumbers. Serve at room temperature.

SPINACH AND MUSHROOMS IN SOY-BUTTER SAUCE

Makes 4½–5 cups

Fresh spinach for six means spending some time washing those sandy spinach leaves. I do think it's worth it—especially if you add a few unusual mushrooms (such as cremini, oyster or shiitake) to the more familiar white ones.

Tip: Wash the spinach early in the day. Cooking will be much easier (and more fun) if that chore is already done.

2½ pounds fresh spinach, thick
    stems discarded, leaves washed
    carefully to remove dirt and sand
    *Note: Shake excess water from
    the spinach leaves, but do not
    pat dry.*

4 tablespoons (½ stick) butter
1 pound mushrooms, trimmed and
    sliced thin
2½ tablespoons soy sauce

1. Tear the spinach in pieces and put as much of it as possible in a large skillet over medium heat. Stir it down as it wilts, adding more spinach until all of it is in the skillet and wilted. Remove the spinach and drain well in a strainer, using a spoon to press out most of the liquid. Discard any liquid left in the skillet.

2. Melt the butter in the skillet. Add the mushrooms and sauté over low heat until they have released their liquid and are limp. Push the mushrooms aside and spoon the mushroom liquid out of the skillet into a bowl; stir the soy sauce into the liquid.

3. Add the spinach to the mushrooms in the skillet and mix well, using a fork and spoon to separate the spinach leaves and combine them with the mushrooms. Pour the soy sauce mixture over the vegetables and stir over low heat until hot. Serve immediately.

Spring Menu #3

Creamy Anchovy Dip with Snow Pea Pods and Endive

SCALLION PANCAKES
WITH SAVORY CHICKEN FILLING

Spicy Red Pepper Sauce
Sweet Tomato Chutney

Fresh pineapple
Brown Sugar Loaf Cake

This is a Sunday night–style supper: not too much food, not too much work—and all of it can be done ahead in stages or at odd moments, if you like. Making the pancakes (which are actually quite easy to prepare) may take a bit of time, but you can do them ahead and store them in the refrigerator or freezer.

Tip: Advice on buying and serving fresh pineapple is on page 20.

NOTES ON THE MENU

To turn this from a light to a hearty supper, serve a sharp cheese and whole-grain crackers along with the dip and vegetables. After the filled pancakes and condiments, bring out a big mixed green salad and plenty of warm Italian or French bread.

CREAMY ANCHOVY DIP WITH SNOW PEA PODS AND ENDIVE

Makes 2 cups of dip

A grown-up dip, so no potato chips, please. For a more substantial appetizer, serve crisp crackers, bread sticks or other vegetables in addition to the snow pea pods and endive.

32–36 anchovy fillets, drained (two 2-ounce cans flat anchovy fillets)
2 cloves garlic, minced
¼ cup water
1¾ cups sour cream

1½ tablespoons fresh lemon juice
Fresh pepper
4 heads Belgian endive, trimmed, leaves separated
½ pound snow pea pods, trimmed

1. In a small skillet, stir together the anchovies, garlic, water and ¼ cup of the sour cream. Bring to a boil, reduce the heat and simmer the mixture, stirring occasionally, for 10 minutes. The mixture will be considerably thickened.

2. Put the anchovy mixture, the remaining 1½ cups sour cream, the lemon juice and a good grinding of pepper in a food processor and process until completely smooth. Cover and chill for 1 hour.

Put the bowl of dip in the center of a serving platter and arrange the endive leaves and snow pea pods around the bowl.

SCALLION PANCAKES WITH SAVORY CHICKEN FILLING

Makes 18–22 pancakes

These are thin pancakes spiked with minced scallions, folded over a lemony chicken and mushroom mixture. Serve with one or both of the condiments suggested here or with your favorite chutney.

Make the batter one hour before making the pancakes. If you like, make the pancakes a day ahead, wrap them well and refrigerate or freeze them until needed. Ditto the chicken filling. You'll need a six- or seven-inch crêpe pan or skillet for making the pancakes.

For the pancakes
½ cup flour
½ cup whole wheat flour
½ teaspoon salt
Fresh pepper
4 eggs, beaten
1½ cups milk
2 tablespoons butter, melted and
   cooled
½ cup minced scallions, green parts
   only
Vegetable oil for browning

For the filling
4 tablespoons (½ stick) butter
1 cup minced mushrooms (about
   3–4 ounces)
   *Note: Cremini mushrooms are
   especially good in this dish.*
Salt
2 cups minced cooked chicken
   (preferably breasts)
2 tablespoons flour
1 cup hot chicken broth
3 tablespoons fresh lemon juice
2 egg yolks stirred with
   1 tablespoon water

1. Make the pancake batter: Stir together the flours, salt and a grinding of pepper. In a separate bowl, whisk together the eggs, milk and melted butter. Gradually add the dry ingredients, stirring until smooth. Add the scallions and stir again. Set the batter aside at room temperature for 1 hour.

2. Make the filling, starting with a chicken mixture: Melt 2 tablespoons of the butter in a skillet. Add the mushrooms, sprinkle with a little salt and stir over low heat until the mushrooms are soft and have given up their liquid. Add the minced chicken and stir well. Use a slotted spoon to transfer the chicken mixture to another bowl. Do not clean the skillet.

3. Now make a lemon sauce: Melt the remaining butter in the skillet, add the flour and stir over low heat for 1 minute. Add the hot broth and lemon juice and stir or whisk until smooth and slightly thickened.

One at a time, stir 3 tablespoons of the hot sauce into the egg yolks to warm them so they don't curdle when you add them to the skillet. Then slowly add the warmed yolks to the skillet and stir or whisk briskly to avoid lumps; the sauce will thicken. Continue cooking and stirring for 1 mor minute.

4. To complete the filling, stir the lemon sauce into the chicken mixture. Taste and season with more salt and pepper if needed. Set aside.

5. Make the pancakes: Heat a little vegetable oil in a 6- or 7-inch crêpe pan or skillet and whirl it around. Stir the batter again.

For each pancake, use ⅙ cup of batter (half of a ⅓-cup measuring cup). Lift the pan off the heat, pour the batter into the hot pan and tilt the pan quickly to spread the batter evenly. Put the pan back on the heat. When the pancake is brown on the bottom and solid-looking on top, about 40 seconds, turn and brown it on the other side (about 30 seconds more). Slide or lift the pancake onto a baking sheet.

Pour a few more drops of oil in the pan. Repeat to make the remaining pancakes, about 20 more. Be sure every pancake has some scallion in it.

Stack the pancakes as they cool. If you like, wrap the cooled pancakes in plastic and refrigerate or freeze until needed. Bring to room temperature before filling.

6. Fill and heat the pancakes: Place 2 level tablespoons of filling just off center on the second (or less pretty) side of each pancake. Fold over and then press gently to spread the filling. Lay the pancakes on a large baking sheet, overlapping as shown. Cover lightly with foil and heat in a 325° oven for 20 minutes.

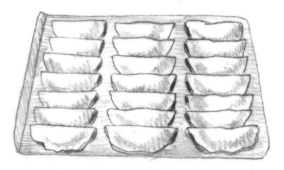

Serve hot with Spicy Red Pepper Sauce and/or Sweet Tomato Chutney.

SPICY RED PEPPER SAUCE

Makes about 1½ cups

3 red bell peppers
1 fresh jalapeño or other hot green
   pepper (optional)

2 tablespoons olive oil
2 tablespoons fresh lime juice
Salt

1. Roast and peel the peppers, including the jalapeño if you are using it (see page 54 for roasting instructions). Remove and discard the seeds and veins and cut the peppers in chunks.

Note: Be careful when handling jalapeños or other hot peppers.

2. Put the pepper chunks, olive oil and lime juice in a food processor and purée. Pour the sauce into a bowl and season with salt to taste.

SWEET TOMATO CHUTNEY

Makes about 1½ cups

2 cups drained canned Italian-style
   whole tomatoes (about one
   35-ounce can)
1 teaspoon minced garlic
1 teaspoon minced ginger
½ cup chopped onion (about
   1 small onion)
½ cup dark or light raisins
¼ cup sugar
½ cup balsamic or red wine vinegar
½ teaspoon salt
¼ teaspoon cayenne pepper or
   ¼ teaspoon hot red pepper
   flakes (optional)

Cut each tomato in half, drain again and then chop coarsely.

Put all the ingredients in a nonreactive saucepan (stainless steel, enameled, etc.) and simmer, uncovered, for 50–60 minutes, or until very thick. Stir often to prevent burning. Season with a little more salt, if needed.

Wedding Lunch or Shower

A light, elegant meal is most appropriate for a traditional wedding or wedding shower. The table should have a light, elegant look, too, with white or pale linen and centerpiece arrangements of airy white flowers and ferns or individual nosegays at each place.

Baked Stuffed Mushrooms (page 88)

Peas and Lettuce Salad with Mustard Dressing (page 40)

Scallion Pancakes with Savory Chicken Filling (pages 28–29)
Cream gravy
Dorothy's Baby Artichokes (page 44)
Cheese Cornmeal Crisps (pages 72–73; make them small)

Strawberries and cream
Grandmother's Sand Cookies (page 22)

BROWN SUGAR LOAF CAKE

Makes 1 loaf cake

Very light, not overly sweet, with a lovely light crumb. Cool the cake completely—it will fall apart if you try to cut it while it's hot. Freezes well.

Tip: Margarine works especially well in this recipe.

1¼ cups flour
½ teaspoon baking soda
1½ teaspoons baking powder
¼ teaspoon salt
¼ teaspoon cinnamon

8 tablespoons (1 stick) butter or margarine, room temperature
½ cup (packed) dark brown sugar
1 egg plus 1 egg yolk
½ cup orange juice

1. Preheat the oven to 350°; grease and flour an 8½ × 4½ × 2½-inch loaf pan.

Stir together the flour, baking soda, baking powder, salt and cinnamon; set aside.

2. In a large bowl, cream the butter. Gradually add the brown sugar, beating well after each addition. Add the egg and egg yolk and beat for 3 minutes.

3. Add the orange juice and dry ingredients alternately, in 3 parts each, start-ing with juice and ending with dry ingredients (in this recipe this is impor-tant); beat well after each addition. Pour the batter into the prepared pan and spread it evenly.

4. Bake for 55–60 minutes, or until a cake tester inserted in the center of the cake comes out clean. Let the cake cool in the pan on a wire rack for 10 min-utes, then carefully turn out to finish cooling, right side up, on the rack.

Biscuit Variations

A basic baking powder or buttermilk biscuit recipe can be enhanced with the addition of one or two simple ingredients. For any standard recipe that yields twelve or eighteen biscuits, try one of the following variations:

• **Bacon biscuits:** Add ¼ cup (or 6 table-spoons) crisp bacon bits before adding liquid to biscuit mix.

• **Cheese biscuits:** Add ½ (or ¾) cup grated cheddar before adding liquid to biscuit mix.

• **Dill biscuits:** Add 1 (or 1½) tablespoons finely minced fresh dill to dry ingredients.

• **Walnut or pecan biscuits:** Add ½ (or ¾) cup finely chopped toasted walnuts or pecans be-fore adding liquid to biscuit mix.

Spring Menu #4

Country-style Sun-dried Tomatoes and Cheese

PAELLA

Orange and Onion Salad

Cinnamon Snaps

A mouth-watering and beautiful dinner and rather challenging, too, because there *are* a lot of steps to making paella. Easy steps, to be sure, but quite a few of them. On the other hand, paella is almost a meal in itself—it needs no more than the simple orange and onion salad to complete the main part of the menu—so it's more efficient than it might appear at first glance.

The appetizer and dessert may be made ahead, so you won't have to worry about them while you're making the main course.

NOTES ON THE MENU

For a more sumptuous dessert, ice cream or sherbet, fresh fruit or fruit salad, Mocha Custard (pages 150–151) or flan would all go well with the cookies.

• **Cinnamon biscuits:** Roll out biscuit dough ¼ inch thick; spread lightly with softened butter and sprinkle with cinnamon sugar. Roll up and cut in 12 (or 18) slices, place slices, cut side down, in a greased muffin tin and sprinkle with a little more cinnamon sugar.

• **Butterscotch biscuits:** Prepare as for cinnamon biscuits, but sprinkle with light brown sugar instead of cinnamon sugar.

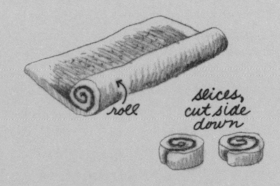

COUNTRY-STYLE SUN-DRIED TOMATOES AND CHEESE

Makes enough for 6

This earthy spread—rough, crunchy, tart and salty all at once—is particularly bracing before a hearty paella. Serve it with plenty of crusty bread.

¼ **pound sun-dried tomatoes**
   Note: Buy dried tomatoes sold in bulk, not jars of sun-dried tomatoes packed in olive oil.
⅓ **pound feta cheese, crumbled**
   Note: If the feta is very salty, soak it for an hour in cold water.
2 **medium stalks celery, trimmed and cut in small dice**

1 **medium carrot, trimmed, peeled and cut in small dice**
1 **clove garlic, minced**
5 **scallions, green parts only, minced**
¼ **cup olive oil**
2 **tablespoons balsamic vinegar**
Fresh pepper
Tabasco or other hot pepper sauce (optional)

1. Put the tomatoes in a small saucepan with water to cover and bring to a boil; simmer just until softened and plumped, about 5 minutes. Drain, rinse and drain again. Pat dry on paper towels. In a food processor or by hand, chop the tomatoes roughly and put them in a large bowl.

2. If you soaked the feta cheese, drain it and spread it on several layers of paper towels; roll up the paper towels to press out the water. Add the crumbled cheese, the celery, carrot, garlic and scallions to the bowl and mix well. Be sure the bits of tomato are well distributed among the other ingredients.

3. Whisk together the olive oil and vinegar and season with pepper and a few dashes of Tabasco, if you like. Pour the dressing on the tomato mixture, toss well and correct seasonings, adding salt if needed.

Spread the tomato mixture on rounds of warm, crusty bread.

PAELLA

Makes plenty for 6, with leftovers

My paella is based on the traditional Spanish dish—an extravaganza of chicken, sausage and shrimp tucked into saffron-flavored rice. It is simply beautiful in its final presentation, studded with red peppers, olives and green peas.

You will need a paella pan or heavy ovenproof skillet (preferably cast iron) at least two inches deep and thirteen inches in diameter, measured across the top.

Note: This method of cooking rice is going to seem peculiar to you but it works like magic.

1 pound chorizo (Spanish-style sausage) or sweet Italian sausage
¼ cup fruity olive oil (preferably Spanish)
8 chicken thighs, boned and halved
2 cups chopped onion (about 2 medium onions)
6 cloves garlic, minced
Salt
Cayenne pepper
Fresh pepper
1 pound large shrimp, shelled and deveined
1½ cups raw long-grain white rice
2¾ cups canned whole tomatoes, with juice (one 28-ounce can)

2 cups chicken broth
2 cups clam juice (two 8-ounce bottles)
¼ teaspoon crumbled saffron
2 cups frozen petite peas, thawed (one 10-ounce package)
2 medium-size red bell peppers, roasted and diced (about 1½ cups)
Note: Roast your own (see page 54) or use roasted peppers from a jar.
½ cup small pitted green olives (one 2¼-ounce jar)

1. If you're using chorizo, cut it in ½-inch slices. If you're using Italian sausage, first prick the sausages all over with a fork. Place in a small skillet with 1 inch of water. Bring to a boil, lower the heat, cover the skillet and let the sausage simmer for 10 minutes, turning once. Cool under cold running water and cut in ½-inch slices.

2. In a large ovenproof skillet or paella pan, brown the sliced sausage. Drain on paper towels and set aside on a platter.

3. Wipe out the pan, add the olive oil and brown the chicken pieces with half the onions and half the garlic, seasoning them with salt, a pinch or two of cayenne pepper and plenty of fresh pepper. Remove the chicken to the platter.

4. Add the shrimp and sauté for 3 minutes, seasoning well with salt and pepper; remove the shrimp to the platter.
Preheat the oven to 325°.

5. Add the remaining onions and garlic to the oil in the pan and sauté until the onion is soft. Add the rice and sauté for 3 minutes, stirring and scraping up the brown bits stuck to the skillet.

6. Add the tomatoes (including the juice), breaking or cutting them up in the pan. Add the broth, clam juice, saffron and peas and bring to a simmer, stirring to dissolve the saffron. Season

well with salt and pepper. Keeping the broth at a simmer, cook for 10 minutes, uncovered, *without stirring*. At this point, the rice will be partially cooked and rather soupy.

7. Arrange the chicken, shrimp and sausage on the rice mixture and push each piece down into the rice; do not stir. The skillet or paella pan will be very full.

8. Scatter the peppers and olives over everything and bake, uncovered, for 15 minutes. Remove from the oven, cover tightly with a lid or with aluminum foil and allow to sit for 10 minutes.
Stir gently and serve hot, right from the skillet or paella pan.

Sangría

This is perfect with Paella. Serve it in a glass pitcher if possible, so your guests get the full visual effect of the fresh fruit.

1 bottle (750 ml) rioja (a dry red table wine from
   Spain) or other dry red wine
1½ cups orange juice
½ cup fresh lemon juice
Superfine sugar
1 navel orange, 1 lemon, 1 lime, small strawberries
   for garnish

In a large pitcher, stir together the wine, orange and lemon juices and sugar to taste. (Don't make sangría overly sweet.) Fill the pitcher with ice cubes.
Cut the orange, lemon and lime in thin slices. Add the sliced fruit and strawberries to the pitcher and stir well.

ORANGE AND ONION SALAD

Makes enough for 6

A refreshing, light salad, to contrast with the heartiness of the paella. Prepare and refrigerate the parts (sliced oranges, sliced onions and shredded lettuce) ahead of time, if you like, then put the salad together and dress it just before serving.

6 navel oranges
1 medium red onion
1 medium-small head of Boston
   lettuce

Salt
Fresh pepper
¼ cup fruity olive oil (preferably
   Spanish)
1 tablespoon balsamic vinegar

1. Carefully peel the orange with a sharp knife, removing all the white pith; cut in slices a little thinner than ¼ inch. Peel the onion and slice it as thin as possible. Wash and dry the lettuce leaves, roll them together a few at a time and cut in narrow strips (makes about 4 cups).

2. Spread the lettuce evenly on a serving platter and sprinkle with salt and pepper. Arrange the orange slices on top, in overlapping concentric rings. Scatter the onion slices on the oranges.

Sprinkle the oranges and onions with salt and freshly ground pepper, then drizzle with the olive oil and vinegar.

    Serve immediately.

scatter onion rings on oranges

CINNAMON SNAPS

Makes about 6½ dozen cookies

Crisp and buttery, with a light cinnamon taste, these cookies really do come close to melting in your mouth. Easy to make, and extras freeze beautifully.

2 cups flour	½ cup sugar
1 teaspoon baking soda	½ cup (packed) dark brown sugar
1 teaspoon cinnamon	1 egg
Pinch of salt	½ teaspoon vanilla extract
8 tablespoons (1 stick) butter, room temperature	¼ cup unsulfured molasses

1. Preheat the oven to 325°; grease 1 or 2 baking sheets.

Stir together the flour, baking soda, cinnamon and salt; set aside.

2. In a large bowl, cream the butter. Gradually add the sugar and brown sugar, beating well after each addition.

3. Add the egg, vanilla and molasses and beat at medium speed for 3 minutes. Add the dry ingredients and blend well. Refrigerate the dough for 1 hour or until firm enough to handle.

4. With well-floured hands, shape the dough into balls about 1 inch in diameter and place them on a prepared baking sheet, leaving 2 inches between them. Flatten each ball with the flour-dusted tines of a fork, pressing down first in one direction and then in the opposite direction.

5. Bake for 12–15 minutes, or until the cookies have puffed and spread; they will deflate and shrink as they cool. Let the cookies cool on the baking sheet on a wire rack for 3 minutes, then remove quickly from the baking sheet and transfer to the rack to finish cooling. Repeat the process with the remaining dough to make as many cookies as you need.

Tip: If you have a second greased baking sheet, fill it while the first batch of cookies is in the oven. Label and freeze any leftover dough or cookies for future use.

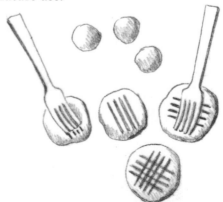

Spring Menu #5

Peas and Lettuce Salad with Mustard Dressing

ROASTED CHICKEN
WITH HERB AND GARLIC BUTTER

Almond-Prune Stuffing
Dorothy's Baby Artichokes

Mango-Lime Tart

An early spring Saturday or Sunday is the perfect occasion for setting a pretty table (see page 49) and inviting guests to celebrate the changing season.

NOTES ON THE MENU

It's not essential, but you may certainly serve a neat pick-up hors d'oeuvre for guests to nibble while they relax before the meal. Try any of the stuffed vegetables on page 100 or one of the appetizers on pages 127 and 128.

Tip: If you don't have time to make everything, serve buttered noodles or barley instead of Almond-Prune Stuffing.

Savory Butters

Savory butters are delicious as spreads for sandwiches or canapés, for sautéing vegetables, for making savory toast, as simple dressings for pasta. Blend or mash the ingredients listed below into one cup (two sticks) of room-temperature sweet butter and refrigerate; use as needed.

- **Mustard Butter:** 1 teaspoon powdered mustard; 2 tablespoons (or more, to taste) prepared mustard

- **Chive Butter:** ¼ cup finely minced fresh chives; ⅛ teaspoon salt; fresh pepper to taste

- **Horseradish Butter:** 2 tablespoons (or more, to taste) prepared horseradish

- **Shallot and Herb Butter:** 4 shallots, quartered; ¼ cup flat-leaf (Italian) parsley leaves; ½ teaspoon crumbled dry oregano; fresh pepper to taste. Blend until smooth.

PEAS AND LETTUCE SALAD WITH MUSTARD DRESSING

Makes enough for 6

Note the new peas and sugar snaps—a real spring salad to whet your appetite for the roasted chicken that follows.

1 pound new green peas in the pod
¼–½ pound sugar snap peas

9–10 cups (loosely packed) bite-size pieces Boston or Bibb lettuce and sprigs of watercress
Mustard Dressing (recipe follows)

1. Shell the new green peas and boil for about 10 minutes or until tender; drain immediately and cool quickly under cold running water. Break the stems off the sugar snap peas and pull to remove the strings.

2. In a large bowl, toss the lettuce and watercress with Mustard Dressing; divide the greens equally among individual salad plates. Sprinkle each with cooked peas and garnish with sugar snap peas.

MUSTARD DRESSING

Makes about 1 cup

¼ cup balsamic, red wine or white wine vinegar
¾ cup vegetable oil
3 tablespoons Dijon-style prepared mustard
1 teaspoon salt
1 teaspoon sugar
Fresh pepper

Blend the ingredients in a food processor or whisk them together by hand, adding fresh pepper to taste.

ROASTED CHICKEN
WITH HERB AND GARLIC BUTTER

Makes plenty for 6

A modest but tasty chicken dish that takes only a short time to prepare. Before roasting, the chickens are butterflied (split and opened out), and a tarragon-flavored butter is rubbed between the skin and the flesh to make the birds moist and juicy.

2 chickens, about 3½ pounds each
4 tablespoons (½ stick) butter,
    room temperature
6 cloves garlic, minced

1 teaspoon dried tarragon,
    powdered
Salt
Fresh pepper

1. Preheat the oven to 375°. Have ready a large roasting pan with a rack.

Butterfly each chicken: Place the chicken, breast down, on a cutting board. Using a cleaver, whack through the backbone (or, if you prefer, snip through the backbone with poultry shears) until it splits and you can open out the chicken. Now, with the inside of the chicken facing up, hack lightly through the wishbone and breastbone (with the cleaver or a heavy knife), just enough to get the butterflied chicken fairly flat. Be careful not to cut all the way through. Pull off and discard any splinters and chips of bone you find along any of the cut edges. Turn the chicken over, skin side up.

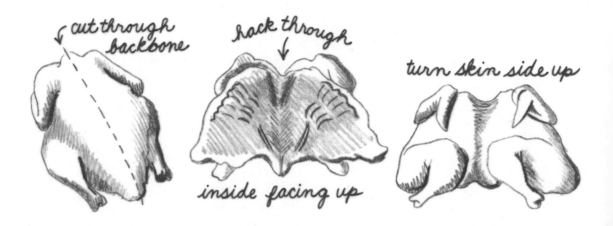

Carefully loosen the skin over the breasts, legs and thighs by sliding your hand between the skin and meat.

2. Mash together the butter, garlic, tarragon, ½ teaspoon of salt and a generous grinding of pepper.

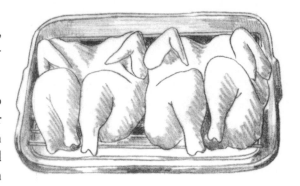

3. Apply half the butter mixture to 1 chicken: With your fingers, smear most of the butter directly on the flesh (under the skin) of the breast, legs and thighs; smear the remaining butter on the skin, including the wings. Repeat with the second half of the butter mixture and the second chicken.

Place the chickens side by side on the roasting pan rack, skin side up, legs and wings on top. Sprinkle with a little more salt.

4. Bake for 1½ hours, basting occasionally, until done. Let the chicken rest for 10 minutes and then carve. Serve hot or warm. If you like, make gravy from the pan drippings.

Easter Dinner

Celebrate with a meal that includes some special spring foods.

Wild Mushrooms on Toast (page 128)

Mixed green salad with spring radishes
Blue Cheese Dressing (page 18)

Roasted Chicken with Tart Orange Sauce (page 102)
Oven-baked Pecan Wild Rice (page 79)
Fresh Asparagus with Browned Shallots (page 20)

Hazelnut Tart with Whipped Cream (page 158)
Chocolate-dipped Strawberries (page 19)

ALMOND-PRUNE STUFFING

Makes about 4½ cups

Frankly, this is one of the best stuffings I know—due to the flavorful whole wheat bread, crunchy almonds and sweet prunes. Of course, no amount of stuffing is enough for true aficionados, but this amount serves six. (If you do want to make more, double the whole recipe and bake it in a larger pan.)

You'll note that I don't suggest baking the stuffing stuffed in the bird. I find it's much better baked in a separate dish in the oven.

8 tablespoons (1 stick) butter
½ cup minced celery
½ cup chopped onion (about
    1 small onion)
¾ cup chopped toasted almonds
    (about ¾ cup whole almonds,
    with or without skins; see page
    23 for toasting instructions)
6 ounces pitted prunes, chopped
2 tablespoons minced flat-leaf
    (Italian) parsley

¼ teaspoon powdered dried sage
¼ teaspoon powdered dried thyme
½ teaspoon salt
Fresh pepper to taste
1 egg beaten with ¾ cup chicken
    broth
5 cups ½-inch cubes whole wheat
    bread, crusts removed first
    (about 15 ounces of premium
    sliced whole wheat bread with
    crusts)

1. Butter a 1½-quart baking dish. Preheat the oven to 375° for an ovenproof glass dish, 400° for non-glass.

Melt the butter in a large skillet over low heat. Add the celery, onion and almonds and sauté until the onion is soft. Turn off the heat and allow the mixture to cool.

2. Add all the remaining ingredients except the bread cubes and stir well. Add the bread cubes and stir again.

3. Pack the stuffing lightly into the prepared baking dish and bake, uncovered, for 35 minutes.

DOROTHY'S BABY ARTICHOKES

Makes enough for 6

Dorothy Berini was a wonderful Italian cook from San Rafael, California, who grumbled while she cooked and left the dishwashing for lesser talents. Dorothy wouldn't, but I do sometimes make the artichokes ahead and reheat them in a skillet or eat them at room temperature.

3 pounds baby artichokes
1½ tablespoons butter
1½ tablespoons olive oil
2½ tablespoons minced shallots
2 or 3 cloves garlic, minced

Salt
3 tablespoons water
Juice of 1 medium lemon
Fresh pepper

1. Prepare the artichokes: Cut off the stem ends close to the globes; peel off leaves until you're down to the ones that are yellow at the stem ends and pale green at the tips; cut off at least ½ inch of the tip of each artichoke.

Note: It may seem like a lot of waste, but you must remove the tough, fibrous leaves and the tops of the inner leaves in order to eat the tender leaves and heart of each baby artichoke.

Cut each baby artichoke in half, from tip to stem end.

Note: It is not necessary to drop the cut artichokes into acidulated water.

2. Melt the butter and oil in a large, nonreactive skillet (stainless steel, enamel, etc.) over medium heat. Add the artichokes, shallots, garlic and a sprinkling of salt and stir well. Cover the skillet and cook, stirring occasionally, for about 10 minutes or until slightly browned on both sides. Turn off the heat.

pull off leaves
trim stem

pale green
yellow
cut off tip
cut in half

3. Add the water and lemon juice, cover the skillet and let the artichokes steam (with the heat off) for 5 minutes. Season with salt and freshly ground pepper, and stir well to get all the browned bits off the bottom of the skillet.

Serve hot or at room temperature.

MANGO-LIME TART

Makes 1 tart

A tart so elegant that it is simply a disk of crisp puff pastry topped with fresh mangoes and lime glaze. Serve it by itself or with vanilla ice cream, or omit the pistachios and serve with butter pecan or butter almond ice cream.

Note: Don't panic—you're not expected to make puff pastry. Use the ready-made, frozen kind.

1 sheet frozen puff pastry (one-half
    16-ounce package)
Cream and sugar for brushing and
    sprinkling on the pastry
2 tablespoons fresh lime juice

2 tablespoons sugar
2 large or 3 medium-size ripe
    mangoes
2 tablespoons chopped unsalted
    pistachio nuts

1. Preheat the oven to 350°.

Thaw and unfold the sheet of puff pastry according to the directions on the package. Roll out the dough just until it is large enough to cut a 10-inch round (trace around a cake or tart pan). Slide the pastry round onto a baking sheet, brush with cream and sprinkle with sugar. Prick the round all over with a fork.

2. Bake for 10 minutes; prick again with a fork or the point of a knife to deflate the pastry. Be sure you push the fork or knife in far enough to let steam escape; you will see the pastry collapse. Bake 15 more minutes, until golden.

Note: During the 15-minute baking period, the pastry may puff up again. If it does, deflate after 10 minutes, then finish baking for 5 more minutes. Total baking time: 25 minutes.

Allow the pastry to cool on the baking sheet and then transfer it to a serving platter.

3. Bring the lime juice and sugar to a boil in a nonreactive saucepan (stainless steel, enameled, etc.) and boil for 1 minute to make a glaze. This glaze, should you happen to taste it, will remind you of lime lollipops. Fortunately, it tastes completely different when brushed on the mangoes.

4. Thinly peel the mangoes. Cut ⅛-inch-thick strips of the flesh, slicing from the stem end to the bottom of the fruit.

Note: Mangoes are not easy to cut, since the flesh is slippery and the pit is large and oddly textured. Just do the best you can.

5. Brush a little of the glaze on the baked pastry. Lay the mango slices on the pastry as neatly as you can, starting at the outer edge and overlapping the slices. Brush lime glaze on the mango slices and sprinkle with the chopped pistachios.

Serve at room temperature, cut in wedges, with or without ice cream.

Beautiful Salads

Tossed salads are wonderful, but sometimes it's fun to serve beautifully arranged raw and cooked vegetables on a bed of crisp greens. Each ingredient is cut in a different—but simple—shape and the pieces arranged neatly. Here are some shapes and arrangements to inspire you.

Spring Menu #6

MARINATED, BAKED ASIAN CHICKEN

Brown Rice with Cashews
Chinese Cabbage Salad

Papaya with Honey-Rum Sauce

Since marinating the chicken and making (but not dressing) the salad can be done ahead, this is a super-easy family supper. And while the chicken is baking, you'll have time to prepare the brown rice and dessert.

NOTES ON THE MENU

To turn this simple supper into a company dinner, begin with an hors d'oeuvre of raw vegetable kebobs to dunk in your favorite dip (or Creamy Anchovy Dip, page 28). Jazz up the main course by offering one sweet and one savory chutney, such as Sweet Tomato Chutney (page 31) and Onion Chutney (page 140).

For dessert, add a light cake or cookies—ladyfingers would be an interesting choice.

MARINATED, BAKED ASIAN CHICKEN

Makes plenty for 6

A richly flavored dish, with plenty of sauce to put on the accompanying rice—Brown Rice with Cashews (page 49) or plain white rice. Start the night before by marinating the chicken.

12 large or 18 small chicken thighs
4-ounce piece ginger, peeled and
    chunked
6 cloves garlic, quartered
¼ cup peanut oil
⅔ cup hoisin sauce
    *Note: Buy hoisin sauce in an
    Asian market or gourmet store.*

¼ cup rice vinegar
¼ cup soy sauce
¼ cup dry sherry
1 teaspoon grated lemon rind
Minced scallions, green parts only,
    for garnish

1. Pierce each chicken thigh 6 or 7 times with a sharp kitchen fork.

Purée the remaining ingredients except the minced scallions in a food processor, to make a marinade. Pour this marinade into a large bowl and add the chicken, turning the pieces to coat well. Cover and leave in the refrigerator overnight or at least 8 hours, turning the pieces occasionally.

2. When you are ready to cook the chicken, preheat the oven to 375°. Arrange the marinated thighs, skin side up, in 1 layer in 1 or 2 large baking dishes (with all the marinade from the bowl) and let them come to room temperature. Bake for 1¼ hours, or until very tender and dark brown.

Arrange the chicken on a platter and serve immediately, garnished with minced scallions, or keep warm in a low oven and garnish with scallions just before serving.

Pour the sauce in the baking dish into a sauceboat and skim off the oil. Serve with the chicken and rice.

BROWN RICE WITH CASHEWS

Makes about 5 cups

Incredibly mellow, a perfect foil for the highly spiced chicken, this rice is also good with vegetable dishes of all kinds. Prepare the rice while the chicken is baking.

6 tablespoons butter or margarine
1½ cups raw brown rice
1¾ cups chicken broth
1¼ cups water

1 cup toasted cashews, chopped
   (see page 23 for toasting
   instructions)
Salt (optional)

1. In a large heavy saucepan, melt the butter (or margarine) over low heat. Add the rice and cook, stirring constantly, for 5 minutes, or until golden brown.

2. Add the broth and water. Stir well, cover the saucepan and cook over very low heat for 45 minutes, or until all (or most of) the liquid is absorbed. Turn off the heat and leave the pan tightly covered for 10 minutes more.

3. Remove the cover and stir in the cashews. Add salt, if needed. Serve immediately or keep warm in a 300° oven.

A Pretty Table Setting for Spring

Lay your table with pastel mats and napkins—pink, green, aqua, yellow, peach, lavender—and set it with white or glass plates.

For your centerpiece, fill baskets with spring flowers—tulips, daffodils, freesia, ranunculus, irises, grape hyacinths. Here's the trick: Cut a block of florist's foam to fit each basket. Dampen the foam and put each block in a double layer of plastic bags, folded down so the flower stems can be pushed into the foam but the plastic won't be seen above the rim of the basket. Tuck green cellophane "grass" around the stems to conceal the florist's foam and plastic bags.

CHINESE CABBAGE SALAD

Makes about 6½ cups

A fresh, bright salad, dressed immediately before serving—it doesn't marinate like some cabbage salads. Be sure to mix well so the cabbage and carrots wilt a little.

1½ pounds Chinese (Napa) cabbage, trimmed, cut in ¾-inch strips and then in squares
3 medium carrots, trimmed, peeled and grated (about 1½ cups)
1 tablespoon sesame seeds
2 tablespoons peanut or vegetable oil
1½ teaspoons sesame oil
2 tablespoons rice vinegar or red wine vinegar
1 tablespoon soy sauce
2 tablespoons honey
½ teaspoon powdered mustard

1. In a large bowl, toss the cabbage and carrots. Toast the sesame seeds in a small skillet, stirring over medium heat for 1 or 2 minutes, until golden brown; set aside.

2. Blend the remaining ingredients in a food processor or blender. Just before serving, pour the dressing on the cabbage mixture, add the toasted sesame seeds and mix for two minutes; the salad will wilt slightly. Serve immediately.

PAPAYA WITH HONEY-RUM SAUCE

Makes 6 servings

Buy firm, ripe golden yellow papayas with speckled skins, or buy them partially ripe and let them finish ripening at home.

2 ripe papayas
¼ cup honey
2 tablespoons rum
1 tablespoon fresh lime juice

1. Thinly peel the papayas with a knife or vegetable peeler. Cut open from stem end to bottom, scoop out and discard the seeds and cut in long, thin slices. Divide the slices and arrange them in fan shapes on 6 dessert plates.

2. In a small saucepan over low heat, stir the honey, rum and lime juice until well blended. Drizzle about 1 tablespoon of sauce over the papaya slices on each plate.

CHAPTER 3

CHICKEN DINNERS FOR SUMMER

Menu #1
GRILLED ROSEMARY CHICKEN

Menu #2
DEVILED CHICKEN SALAD
WITH GRUYÈRE CHEESE

Menu #3
BEER-BATTER-FRIED CHICKEN DRUMSTICKS

Menu #4
CALIFORNIA CHICKEN SALAD
WITH CREAMY LIME DRESSING

Menu #5
CHICKEN MILANAISE

Menu #6
HERB AND SPICE CHICKEN BAKED IN FOIL

Chicken is a perfect summer food, with a variety of hot-weather advantages. As you'll see from the recipes in these six dinners, chicken can be made into cold salad, grilled outdoors or quickly sautéed (to avoid heating up the whole house), or even cooked in the cool of the evening and served the following day. And if there's any chicken left over, it's ready-made for the next afternoon's cold lunch. Of course, you need not trust to chance in the matter of leftovers: Prepare a double recipe of your favorite chicken dish and freeze the extra to serve on a night when you'd rather not cook. (This is especially good conservation strategy, since you'll get two meals for the cost of heating the stovetop or oven only once.)

Here's more good news for summer: It takes only thirty minutes to prepare poached chicken breasts (fifteen minutes with the heat on and fifteen minutes with the heat off; see page 13)—and poached chicken is the basis for two of the menus and for a lot of great chicken sandwiches (see page 80).

Fresh produce is at a glorious peak in summer, too, so these dinners are chock-full of the best seasonal fruits and vegetables—tomatoes, corn, fresh herbs, peaches, raspberries, melon and much more.

Note: Remember that dishes listed in *italics* on the menus do not have accompanying recipes.

Summer Menu #1

Parmesan Toast
Mixed green salad with sliced Kirby cucumbers
Garlic Vinaigrette Sauce (page 95)

GRILLED ROSEMARY CHICKEN

Creamy Pasta with Roasted Yellow Peppers

Cold honeydew melon with lime wedges
One-Bowl Sour Cream Chocolate Chip Cake

A leisurely meal with no last-minute, rushed preparation. Everything can be made ahead, stored appropriately until dinner time and then served either at room temperature (if that's easiest) or otherwise—toast hot, salad chilled, chicken warm, honeydew cold.

NOTES ON THE MENU

Since you're grilling the chicken anyway, adding Grilled Summer Vegetables (page 66) is an easy way to expand the menu for a more elaborate dinner or party buffet. Also, you might precede the salad with an hors d'oeuvre of cold smoked salmon with lemon, capers and chopped onions on thin buttered slices of black bread.

Mix-and-Match Menus

Cool Tomato-Basil Soup (page 59)

Chicken Milanaise (pages 76–77)
Grilled Summer Vegetables (pages 66–67)
French or Italian bread

Fresh Raspberry Sundae
with Brandied Chocolate Sauce (page 62)

Baby Green Beans and Fresh Tomatoes
with Sweet-Sour Dressing (page 78)

Herb and Spice Chicken Baked in Foil
(pages 83–84)
Black and White Beans (page 72)

Peaches or Nectarines
with Blueberry Sauce (page 73)
Almond Crunch Cookies (page 68)

PARMESAN TOAST

Makes 18–24 slices

Make ahead if you like, then warm this savory toast in a low oven before serving. Use high-quality cheese, preferably freshly grated.

4 tablespoons (½ stick) butter, room temperature
2 tablespoons grated Parmesan cheese or a combination of Parmesan and Romano cheeses

2 tablespoons flat-leaf (Italian) parsley leaves
8–10 fresh basil leaves
½ clove garlic
18–24 one-inch-thick slices of Italian bread

1. Preheat the broiler.

Put all the ingredients except the bread in a food processor and process until completely smooth.

2. Toast the bread on 1 side. Spread flavored butter on the untoasted side of each piece and place them, butter side up, on a baking sheet. Run the toast under the broiler just long enough to crisp it. Serve hot.

How to Roast a Fresh Pepper

The best way to roast a pepper is over a gas flame (the burner of a gas stove). Char the thin skin of the pepper all over without letting the flesh become too soft. (Roasting on a baking sheet under the oven broiler results in uneven charring and overcooked peppers; do it only if you have no flame.)

Impale the pepper on a long kitchen fork and pull up a chair—this takes a few minutes. Hold the pepper over a medium flame and let the flame blacken the skin. Turn as each area blackens, and reposition the pepper on the fork when necessary so the flame eventually reaches every part. When blackening is complete, pop the hot pepper into a colander in the sink. Leave it there while you char any additional peppers. (Do not put the charred peppers in a plastic or paper bag, as this will steam and overcook them; they will be just as easy to peel without steaming.)

When all the peppers are done, run cold water over them while you rub away the blackened skin. The skin will come off easily and the colander will catch the bits of charred skin. Pat dry and use according to your needs.

GRILLED ROSEMARY CHICKEN

Makes plenty for 6, with leftovers

The trick to making great grilled chicken is to marinate it overnight, precook it in the oven (this is important) and then finish it—for flavor and crispness—on the grill.

Note: Once the chicken is grilled, either eat it or put it away in the refrigerator until serving. Do not leave it out in the summer heat.

1½ cups olive oil
½ cup water
½ cup red or white wine vinegar
2 cloves garlic, quartered

2 tablespoons minced fresh
  rosemary leaves, or
  1⅓ tablespoons crumbled
  dry rosemary
1 teaspoon salt
Fresh pepper to taste
7–8 pounds chicken quarters

1. Make the marinade: Put all ingredients except the chicken in a food processor and process until well blended and almost smooth. Taste and add more salt and pepper if necessary. Reserve 1 cup of the marinade.

2. Put the chicken quarters in a large baking dish, stainless steel roasting pan or shallow casserole. Pour the unreserved marinade over them and turn the pieces to make sure they are thoroughly coated. Cover and refrigerate overnight or for 8–10 hours, turning 2 or 3 times.

3. When you are ready to cook the chicken, take it out of the refrigerator and pour out and discard the marinade. Arrange the chicken in 1 layer in 1 or 2 baking dishes. Place the dish or dishes in the oven (no preheating needed for this recipe), turn the temperature to 400° and bake for 45 minutes.

Note: While it doesn't matter with stainless steel or other metals, a cold glass or ceramic baking dish must start the cooking process in a cold oven so it heats gradually as the oven heats, eliminating the chance of breakage due to sudden temperature changes.

Meanwhile, prepare the grill, allowing at least 30–40 minutes for the coals to burn until they become ash-covered.

4. Grill the partially cooked chicken, turning several times and basting often with the reserved cup of marinade, for 10–20 minutes, or until the chicken is thoroughly cooked and browned or charred the way you like it. Place the grilled chicken on a clean platter and serve immediately or refrigerate until needed.

CREAMY PASTA
WITH ROASTED YELLOW PEPPERS

Makes about 10 cups

This is a lot of pasta salad, but since it's usually most convenient to cook all of a one-pound box of dried pasta, you'll just have to enjoy the leftover salad. If you like, prepare the parts of the salad ahead—but do not combine them until an hour before serving.

1½ cups chicken broth
1¼ cups white wine
1 cup heavy cream
1 pound dried small pasta shells

3 medium-size yellow bell peppers, roasted and peeled (see page 54)
¾ cup Kalamata olives (about ⅓ pound)
Salt
Fresh pepper

1. Combine the broth, wine and cream in a heavy saucepan and simmer briskly, uncovered, over medium heat until reduced to 1½ cups of sauce. Set the sauce aside in the refrigerator.

2. Meanwhile, prepare the rest of the ingredients: Cook the pasta in a large pot of salted or unsalted boiling water, until al dente, about 7 minutes. Drain well and run plenty of cold water over the pasta to cool it. Drain again, tossing it with your hands to shake the water out.

Remove the stems, seeds and veins from the roasted peppers. Cut the flesh in ⅛-inch strips; cut the strips in half.

Pit the olives and dice the flesh (about ½ cup diced).

3. One hour before serving, stir together the pasta, peppers, olives and cream sauce. Season to taste with salt and freshly ground pepper. Serve cool (not cold) or at room temperature.

ONE-BOWL SOUR CREAM CHOCOLATE CHIP CAKE

Makes 1 tube cake

A delectable sour cream cake that won't have a chance to get stale because it will disappear so fast. You'll need a nine-inch-diameter fluted tube pan (also called a kugelhopf pan) for this easy-to-make cake.

1½ cups flour
2 teaspoons baking powder
½ teaspoon baking soda
Pinch of salt
1 cup sugar

4 tablespoons (½ stick) butter,
  very soft
2 eggs
½ cup sour cream
1 teaspoon vanilla extract
¾ cup miniature chocolate chips

1. Preheat the oven to 375°; grease and flour a 9-inch-diameter fluted tube pan.

In a large bowl, whisk together the flour, baking powder, baking soda, salt and sugar.

2. Add the butter, eggs, sour cream and vanilla and beat at low speed just until all the ingredients are dampened. Beat at high speed until very smooth; the butter should be thoroughly incorporated. Stir in the chocolate chips.

Pour and spoon the batter into the prepared pan and spread it evenly with a spatula.

3. Bake for 50 minutes, or until a tester inserted in the cake comes out clean. Let the cake cool in the pan on a wire rack for 10 minutes, then turn out to finish cooling, right side up, on the rack.

Summer Menu #2

Cool Tomato-Basil Soup

DEVILED CHICKEN SALAD WITH GRUYERE CHEESE

Onion Biscuits

Fresh Raspberry Sundae with Brandied Chocolate Sauce

For a hot summer night, a refreshingly cold meal. Make the soup ahead so it has time to chill. You may want to poach the chicken and bake the biscuits the night before, too, when temperatures are bearable.

Tip: If you like, chill the soup bowls in the refrigerator and the ice cream dishes in the freezer.

NOTES ON THE MENU

This menu would make a perfect luncheon just as it is but served in smaller portions; the amounts will be just right for eight people. You might choose to make the biscuits a little smaller, too, following the old-fashioned luncheon tradition.

Setting a Summer Garden Table

If you have a blue and white large-check tablecloth, set your table with:

- Crisp white napkins and a centerpiece of brilliantly colored zinnias
- Lemon-yellow napkins and little glasses or vases full of yellow-centered white daisies
- Flower-print napkins and baskets of dahlias

COOL TOMATO-BASIL SOUP

Makes about 6½ cups

Fresh tomatoes plus fresh basil is one of the best flavor combinations of summer. Serve this soup cool but not so cold that you can't taste it.

2¾–3 pounds ripe tomatoes
1 clove garlic, quartered
½ cup chopped onion (about
    1 small onion)
1¾ cups chicken broth
1 5-ounce can evaporated milk

1 tablespoon sugar
2 tablespoons chopped fresh basil
Salt
Fresh pepper
Fresh basil leaves for garnish

1. Peel the tomatoes: Immerse the tomatoes in boiling water for about 45 seconds; rinse under cold water. Slit the skins (if they haven't already split open) and slip them off.

Core the tomatoes, then cut in half across and gently squeeze out the juice and seeds through a strainer set over a bowl. Reserve the tomatoes and juice; discard the seeds.

2. Purée half the tomatoes with the tomato juice, garlic, onion, broth, milk and sugar. Pour the soup into a large bowl or tureen.

3. Chop the remaining tomatoes and stir them into the soup, with the chopped basil and salt and pepper to taste.

Chill the soup until it is cool (but not icy) and ladle it into bowls. Garnish each bowl with several small basil leaves.

If you have a simple white tablecloth, set your table with:

- Apple-green napkins and a centerpiece of trailing ivy and any white flowers
- Red and white striped or checked napkins and a pot or two of red and white striped petunias
- Pink napkins and white china pitchers full of pink roses

DEVILED CHICKEN SALAD
WITH GRUYERE CHEESE

Makes about 6 cups

Baby green beans add a lovely crunch to this hearty French salad with a creamy tarragon dressing. The flavor of the dressing is subtle, so eat the salad at room temperature or just slightly chilled.

½ **pound baby green beans, stem ends trimmed**
3 **whole chicken breasts, poached, skinned, boned and cut in ½-inch pieces (see page 13 for poaching instructions)**
⅓ **pound Gruyère cheese, grated (about 1½ cups)**

For the dressing
3 **tablespoons white wine**
¾ **cup sour cream**
¼ **cup mayonnaise**
2 **tablespoons Dijon-style prepared mustard**
Note: Other French, German

and whole-grain mustards work well, too; do not use hot dog mustard.
1 **teaspoon powdered dried tarragon**
Salt
Fresh pepper

6 **cups (loosely packed) bite-size pieces of salad greens, such as Boston and red leaf lettuce, arugula and watercress**
Cornichons (or dill pickle cut in matchsticks), small radishes and niçoise olives for garnish

1. Blanch the beans for 1 minute. Drain, rinse in cold water and drain again; pat dry on paper towels. Cut in 1½-inch lengths.

In a large bowl, toss the chicken with the beans and all but 1 cup of the grated cheese.

2. Make the dressing: Whisk together all the dressing ingredients, including salt to taste and a good grinding of pepper. Pour ¾ cup of the dressing on the chicken mixture and toss well. Taste and add more dressing if you like. (At this point, you may refrigerate the salad overnight, if necessary.)

Note: Tasted alone, the dressing may seem bitter; mixed into the salad, it smooths out and blends perfectly with the ingredients.

3. Arrange the greens on a platter. Mound the chicken salad in the center and surround with the remaining Gruyère cheese, cornichons, radishes and olives. Top with a radish flower or other garnish.

ONION BISCUITS

Makes 18–20 biscuits

Crisp on the outside, tender on the inside, studded with bits of browned onion and topped with butter and Parmesan cheese. These unusual biscuits are absolutely adored by everyone who tastes them—and they are easy to make, too.

1 tablespoon butter or margarine for browning the onions	**1 teaspoon salt**
1½ cups minced onion (about 2 medium onions)	**⅓ cup (5⅓ tablespoons) cold margarine, sliced in pats**
2 cups flour	**⅔ cup milk**
2½ teaspoons baking powder	**½ tablespoon butter, melted**
	Grated Parmesan cheese

1. Preheat the oven to 450°.

In a medium skillet, melt the first tablespoon of butter (or margarine), add the onions and sauté slowly, until all the bits are soft and brown. Set aside to cool.

2. In a food processor, mix the flour, baking powder and salt. Add the cold pats of margarine and process until the mixture resembles cornmeal. Turn out into a bowl, add the onions and stir until the bits are separated and coated with flour. Stir in enough of the milk to form a slightly sticky ball of dough.

3. Turn out the dough onto a flour-dusted board and, with floured hands, knead lightly about 10 times. Roll or pat out the dough to ½ inch thick. Cut with a 2-inch round cutter and place the biscuits on wax paper. Reknead the excess dough and repeat the process.

Brush the tops of the biscuits with the melted butter and sprinkle with Parmesan cheese.

4. Place the biscuits on an ungreased baking sheet and bake on the middle shelf of the oven for 25–35 minutes, depending on how you like your biscuits: After 25 minutes, they will be crisp on top and very moist inside; after 35 minutes, they will be very crisp all over and drier (though still moist) inside.

Serve immediately or set aside until needed; reheat the biscuits in a low oven before serving.

FRESH RASPBERRY SUNDAE WITH BRANDIED CHOCOLATE SAUCE

Makes 6 servings

Glass dishes make a nice presentation for this dessert, but any pretty dessert bowls will do. Have the raspberries and warm chocolate sauce ready and make the dessert at the last moment, of course.

2 cups fresh raspberries
Brandied Chocolate Sauce (recipe follows)

Vanilla ice cream

1. Gently crush the raspberries just enough to reduce them to 1¼ cups. Warm the chocolate sauce in a small saucepan over very low heat or in a bowl over a saucepan of simmering water.

2. For each sundae, put a scoop of vanilla ice cream in a bowl and top with 3 tablespoons of the crushed raspberries. Spoon about 2 tablespoons of the warm Brandied Chocolate Sauce over the berries and serve immediately.

BRANDIED CHOCOLATE SAUCE
Makes about 1 cup

2 squares (2 ounces) unsweetened chocolate, chopped
2 squares (2 ounces) semisweet chocolate, chopped
¼ cup light corn syrup
¼ cup sugar
2 tablespoons butter
Pinch of salt
3 tablespoons brandy
1½ tablespoons water
½ teaspoon vanilla extract

Put all the ingredients in a small saucepan over very low heat and stir until the butter and chocolate melt and the sugar is dissolved. Serve warm.

To store the sauce, spoon it into a heatproof jar or crock and allow to cool; cover and refrigerate until needed. Warm the sauce in a saucepan over very low heat or in a bowl over a saucepan of simmering water.

Summer Menu #3

My Favorite Stuffed Eggs

BEER-BATTER-FRIED CHICKEN DRUMSTICKS

Grilled Summer Vegetables
Corn on the cob

Watermelon
Almond Crunch Cookies

This is a great menu for that Fourth of July party around the backyard grill. As with many grilling menus, the last-minute recipes are best executed by two cooks—one in the kitchen frying chicken and preparing corn and one at the grill doing the vegetables.

Tip: If it's too hot in the kitchen to cook during the day, fry the chicken the evening before the party, when it's cooler, and serve the chicken cold the following day.

NOTES ON THE MENU

When several cooks are participating in the preparations, it's fun to do a few traditional American desserts for this traditional American holiday—perhaps strawberry shortcake, layer cake, blueberry pie or homemade ice cream.

MY FAVORITE STUFFED EGGS

Makes 18 appetizers

Traditional picnic fare. Make the stuffed eggs ahead if you like, but keep them covered and refrigerated until serving time.

10 hard-boiled eggs, shelled
3 tablespoons mayonnaise
2 tablespoons half-and-half or
   cream

1½ tablespoons Dijon-style
   prepared mustard
¼ cup finely chopped cornichons
Parsley leaves, paprika and whole
   capers for garnish

1. Slice 9 of the eggs in half lengthwise. Gently remove the yolks and put them in a bowl with the remaining egg. Set aside the whites. Mash the yolks and the whole egg.

2. Add the remaining ingredients except the garnishes and blend well.

3. Spoon the yolk mixture into the hollow of each egg white, using dampened fingers to shape the mounds neatly. Decorate each stuffed egg with a parsley leaf, a pinch of paprika and 2 or 3 capers, as shown in the drawing.

Quick Summer Appetizers

• Carefully slice off and discard the top crust of a ripe Brie or Camembert cheese. Decorate the creamy top with a selection of minced fresh herbs and vegetables (parsley, basil, dill, peppers, olives, capers, etc.). Serve with crackers or toast.

• Core, chop and drain 1 large tomato. Stir in a bowl with 1 chopped, ripe, black-skinned (Hass) avocado, the juice of ½ lime, 1 teaspoon or more finely minced hot green pepper (optional), 1 minced scallion, 2 tablespoons minced fresh coriander and ¼ cup mayonnaise. Serve with tortilla chips.

• Serve blanched fresh green beans, bell pepper strips, cherry tomatoes and thick-sliced mushrooms with garlic mayonnaise dip.

• Roll narrow strips of thin-sliced ham or Italian salami around tiny sweet pickles and skewer each on a toothpick with a cube of Edam cheese.

BEER-BATTER-FRIED CHICKEN DRUMSTICKS

Makes plenty for 6

Follow the instructions carefully and you'll have perfectly fried chicken—crisp but not greasy, thoroughly cooked but still moist. Delicious right out of the pan (and oven) but also great when made ahead.

3 eggs, separated
4 tablespoons (½ stick) butter, melted and cooled
¾ cup flat beer

1½ cups flour stirred with ¼ teaspoon salt
18 chicken drumsticks
Vegetable oil (not olive oil)

1. In a medium bowl, beat together the egg yolks, melted butter and beer. Gradually add the flour, stirring just until the batter is smooth. Cover and refrigerate for at least 3 hours. Don't cheat on this step—the refrigeration time is important.

2. When you are ready to cook the chicken, do the following: Let the drumsticks come to room temperature and pat them completely dry. Preheat the oven to 325°. Beat the egg whites until they hold soft peaks, then fold them into the batter. Pour oil into a large skillet to a depth of ½ inch; heat to 350° or until a cube of bread dropped in the oil browns in 65 seconds.

3. Put 6 drumsticks in the batter and turn each until coated. One at a time, lift the drumsticks out of the bowl, use a soft pastry brush to remove any excess batter and place the batter-coated drumsticks in the pan. Brown for 14 minutes—7 minutes on the first side, 5 minutes on the opposite side, 2 minutes on the third side. (It sounds improbable that a drumstick should have 3 sides, but you'll see when you start frying that it does work out that way.) Drain on paper towels.

Repeat to fry the remaining drumsticks in 2 more batches, adding more oil if needed and reheating the oil to the proper temperature between batches.

Place all the drumsticks on a baking sheet in the oven for 10 minutes to finish cooking. Serve hot or cold.

GRILLED SUMMER VEGETABLES

Makes plenty for 6

I'm a city dweller, so I don't get to grill as often as I'd like. When I do, these herb-and-oil-brushed vegetables are my favorites.

Tip: Prepare a variety of vegetables—and consider including some you haven't tried before.

Selection of vegetables from the list in step 1, prepared and cut into pieces as described
Note: As suggested in step 1, *have at least 30–36 pieces ready for grilling.*
Seasoned Olive Oil (recipe follows)

1. Select the vegetables you like from the list below, and prepare and cut them up as described. Allow at least 5 or 6 vegetable pieces per person, depending on the size of the pieces and the appetites of your guests.

Longer-cooking vegetables:

Eggplant: Trim tops and tails; slice in ¾-inch-thick rounds.

Fennel: Trim root end and cut off top; cut in ¾-inch slices through root end. Some slices will fall apart; grill those pieces, too.

Onions: Peel medium or large red or yellow onions and cut in ¾-inch slices.

Pattypan squash: Trim stem end. Cut in half crosswise if large; do not cut if small.

Shorter-cooking vegetables:

Belgian endive: Remove wilted outer leaves; cut in half lengthwise.

Mushrooms (large): Trim stems almost to cap; leave whole.

Peppers: If small, leave whole; if large, may be left whole or may be stemmed, quartered and seeded.

Radicchio: Remove wilted outer leaves; cut in half through stem end.

Summer squash (yellow): Trim tops and tails; cut in half lengthwise.

Zucchini: Trim tops and tails; cut in half lengthwise.

2. Brush the vegetable pieces generously all over with Seasoned Olive Oil and, keeping them in separate groups, pile them on a large ovenproof platter or roasting pan.

3. Make sure your grill rack is very clean, then heat your grill as usual until the coals are covered with ash. Place the longer-cooking vegetables on the grill first, let them get a good start and then add the shorter-cooking ones. As the pieces cook, pay close attention to their progress so you can turn them when necessary, to achieve uniform doneness and browning.

Remove each piece when it is done, placing it on the platter or roasting pan; reheat all the vegetables in a hot oven for just a few minutes before serving.

SEASONED OLIVE OIL
Makes about 1½ cups

How much you need depends on how many vegetables you are grilling; the amount given here is enough for vegetables for six people. Make the seasoned oil at least a few hours before you'll need it, giving the flavor time to develop.

1¼ cups fruity olive oil
1 or 2 cloves garlic
¼ teaspoon hot red pepper flakes
5 tablespoons (packed) roughly
    chopped fresh basil

2 tablespoons snipped fresh chives
1½ teaspoons salt
Fresh pepper to taste

Blend all the ingredients in a food processor.

ALMOND CRUNCH COOKIES

Makes 7 dozen cookies

A very easily made cookie (especially when the dough is prepared in advance and stashed in the freezer or refrigerator) with a warm, toasted almond flavor. Seven dozen is a lot of cookies—you may want to freeze half the dough or half the cookies for another time.

2 cups flour
½ teaspoon baking powder
¼ teaspoon salt
¾ cup toasted almonds, finely chopped (see page 23 for toasting instructions)

12 tablespoons (1½ sticks) butter, room temperature
½ cup sugar
½ cup (packed) light brown sugar
1 egg
1 teaspoon vanilla extract
½ teaspoon almond extract

1. Stir together the flour, baking powder, salt and chopped almonds. Set aside.

2. In a large bowl cream the butter, sugar and brown sugar. Add the egg and vanilla and almond extracts and beat well, until light.

3. Add the dry ingredients and blend well. Refrigerate the dough until firm, about 1 hour.

When the dough is firm, divide in half, dust your hands with flour and shape each piece into a log about 2 inches in diameter. Wrap snugly in plastic, label each log and refrigerate again until firm. (You may also refrigerate or freeze the dough for later use.)

4. When you are ready to bake the cookies, preheat the oven to 350° and grease a baking sheet. Unwrap the dough and cut as many ⅛-inch-thick slices as will fit on the prepared baking sheet, leaving 1 inch between cookies.

Bake for 12–13 minutes, or until lightly browned; the cookies will be a bit soft on top, but they firm up as they cool. Let the cookies cool for 1 minute on the baking sheet, then transfer to wire racks to finish cooling.

Repeat the process to bake as many cookies as you want, without greasing the baking sheet again unless really necessary. Return any leftover dough to the freezer for future use.

Summer Menu #4

CALIFORNIA CHICKEN SALAD
WITH CREAMY LIME DRESSING

Black and White Beans
Cheese Cornmeal Crisps

Peaches or Nectarines with Blueberry Sauce

Listless summer appetites promptly revive when you serve this tempting meal. It's particularly pleasing to the eye, with the visual impact of the black and white beans, the beautiful presentation of the salad and the contrast of the rich yellow fruit topped with dark sauce.

NOTES ON THE MENU

To jazz up the dessert, serve the sliced fruit and sauce on slices of sponge or pound cake or in tartlet shells.

Grilled Chicken Kebobs

Marinate cubes of boneless chicken for 3–4 hours in the refrigerator in this marinade: ½ cup white wine or dry vermouth; ¼ cup olive oil; juice of one lime; one clove garlic, minced or pressed; one teaspoon crumbled dried tarragon or rosemary; ½ teaspoon salt; fresh pepper.

Thread the marinated chicken cubes on metal skewers with any of the following combinations (brushed with oil and herbs first, if you like). Grill the kebobs for 10–12 minutes or until thoroughly cooked, turning as needed.

• Small whole peeled onions, squares of bell pepper, mushroom caps, chunks of zucchini or pattypan squash, chunks of eggplant

• Squares of bell pepper and red onion; cubed pineapple added for the last few minutes of grilling

• Small whole peeled onions and chunks of parboiled sausage; small figs added for the last few minutes of grilling

CALIFORNIA CHICKEN SALAD WITH CREAMY LIME DRESSING

Makes about 5 cups

Rich, satisfying, filling. Try a mild or spicy chutney as a sophisticated accompaniment to this salad.

½ pound sliced bacon, cooked crisp
   and drained on paper towels
2 firm, ripe black-skinned (Hass)
   avocados
3 whole chicken breasts, poached,
   skinned, boned and cut in
   ½-inch pieces (see page 13 for
   poaching instructions)
3 medium scallions, white and
   green parts, minced (about
   ¼ cup)
Creamy Lime Dressing (recipe
   follows)
Salt

Leaves of 2 small or 1 medium
   head of tender lettuce, such as
   Bibb or Boston
12–15 red or yellow cherry
   tomatoes, halved, for garnish

Summer Fruit Desserts

• Pare the skin from a cantaloupe and cut across in thick slices, discarding the seeds. Place a slice on each plate and fill the center with vanilla ice cream or frozen yogurt. Top with berries and a spoonful of orange or other fruit liqueur.

1. Chop or crumble the bacon; reserve 2 tablespoons. Cut the avocados in half; set aside 1 half with the pit still in it. Peel the remaining 3 halves and cut the flesh into ½-inch pieces.

2. Put the chicken, bacon (except the reserved 2 tablespoons), avocado pieces and scallions in a large bowl. Add about 1½ cups of the Creamy Lime Dressing and toss the salad lightly but thoroughly. Add salt to taste and more dressing, too, if needed. (At this point you may cover and refrigerate the chicken salad until serving time.)

3. Arrange the lettuce leaves to cover a serving platter. Mound the chicken salad neatly in the center, with a 2-inch border of lettuce; sprinkle the reserved bacon on the chicken. Place the cherry tomatoes on the lettuce. Slice the reserved avocado and arrange like petals on the chicken salad, with a cherry tomato in the center.

Any leftover Creamy Lime Dressing may be served with the salad.

CREAMY LIME DRESSING
Makes about 2½ cups

1½ cups mayonnaise
½ cup sour cream
2 tablespoons fresh lime juice
2 tablespoons milk or cream
2 teaspoons sugar
Salt

Whisk the ingredients together, adding salt to taste.

• Toss sliced plums and nectarines in a little port wine. Arrange in fan shapes on giant vanilla or chocolate cookies from the bakery and add a small scoop of raspberry sherbet.

• Peel freestone peaches (immerse in boiling water for 45 seconds; rinse immediately in cold water; peel) and cut in half. Discard the pits and scoop out the stringy fibers from the centers. Fill the centers with orange marmalade or apricot jam, top with sweetened whipped cream or with sour cream and sprinkle with chopped toasted almonds.

BLACK AND WHITE BEANS

Makes about 5½ cups

The dense texture of beans, dressed with vinaigrette and lightly flavored with fresh dill and a crunch of red pepper, makes a good contrast to the creamy California Chicken Salad.

2 cups canned small white beans (one 1-pound can)
4 cups canned black beans (two 1-pound cans)
½ cup Garlic Vinaigrette Sauce (page 95)
1 tablespoon minced fresh dill

2 tablespoons minced flat-leaf (Italian) parsley
1 red bell pepper, seeded, deveined and minced (about 1 cup)
Salt
Fresh pepper

1. Rinse and drain the beans in a colander. In a large bowl, stir together the remaining ingredients except salt and pepper.

2. Add the beans, mix thoroughly and season to taste with salt and pepper. Cover and allow to marinate for 1 hour, stirring occasionally.

Serve cold or at room temperature.

CHEESE CORNMEAL CRISPS

Makes 18–20 crisps

Absolutely delicious—as tasty as cornbread but shaped like pancakes, crisp all over and tender in the middle, with a mild cheese flavor. Serve in a napkin-lined basket or bowl.

½ cup yellow cornmeal
½ cup flour
¼ teaspoon salt
2 teaspoons sugar
1½ teaspoons baking powder
¾ cup grated cheddar cheese (about 2–3 ounces)

1 egg
2 tablespoons margarine or butter, melted and cooled
10 tablespoons (½ cup plus 2 tablespoons) milk

1. Preheat the oven to 425°; grease 2 baking sheets.

In a large bowl, whisk together the cornmeal, flour, salt, sugar and baking powder. Add the grated cheese and toss with your fingers to separate and coat the cheese bits with the cornmeal mixture.

2. Beat the egg and melted margarine or butter into the milk and add the milk mixture to the dry ingredients. Stir until smooth, then let the batter rest for 15 minutes.

3. Drop rounded tablespoons of batter onto the prepared baking sheets, leaving 3 inches between mounds. With a spoon or the tip of a small spatula, spread the batter into 3-inch rounds.

4. Bake the 2 sheets side by side or on the 2 center shelves of the oven for 8–9 minutes, until the crisps are browned on 1 side. Use a spatula to turn all the crisps, pushing the spatula firmly under each one to loosen it from the baking sheet, and then reverse the baking sheets —bottom sheet to the upper shelf, top sheet to the lower shelf. Bake for 7–8 more minutes, or until golden brown. Transfer the crisps to a wire rack.

Cool the baking sheets, then grease again and repeat the process with any remaining batter.

PEACHES OR NECTARINES WITH BLUEBERRY SAUCE

Makes plenty for 6; about 2 cups of sauce

Ripe, juicy summer fruit is just about perfect on its own for lunch, but blueberry sauce dresses it up handsomely for dinner.

2 cups blueberries, picked over and
    rinsed (about 1 pint)
¼ cup water
½ cup sugar

1 tablespoon fresh lemon juice
6 large or 8 medium-size ripe
    peaches or nectarines, peeled or
    unpeeled

1. To make the sauce: Purée 1 cup of the berries. In a heavy saucepan over medium heat, combine the puréed blueberries, water, sugar and lemon juice and simmer for 15 minutes. Turn off the heat and stir in the remaining blueberries. Let the sauce cool.

2. Cut the peaches or nectarines in half, discard the pits and scoop out any hard or stringy matter remaining in the centers. Slice neatly and arrange on a serving platter or in a bowl. Drizzle some of the sauce on the fruit and pass the rest when you serve the fruit.

Summer Menu #5

Chilled Corn Soup

CHICKEN MILANAISE

**Baby Green Beans and Fresh Tomatoes with Sweet-Sour Dressing
Oven-baked Pecan Wild Rice**

Apricots with Ricotta Cream
Crisp cookies

Here's a company menu, guaranteed to please any group of sophisticated diners gathered around your table. But I assure you that the meal is not at all difficult to prepare—it's the simple elegance and freshness that will impress them.

NOTES ON THE MENU

The menu is a bit elaborate for an ordinary weekday dinner, so feel free to simplify it for the family: Omit the corn soup (which, by the way, is delicious for lunch); serve sliced tomatoes instead of the beans-and-tomatoes salad; finish with whole ripe apricots and cookies for dessert.

Cool Summer Drinks

Serve summer drinks in tall glasses (rinsed, then chilled in the freezer for a real treat), with appropriate garnishes of mint leaves, berries, chunks of fresh fruit on wooden skewers, thin slices of orange and lemon. Be sure you have plenty of ice on hand. Here is a reminder list of summer drinks:

• Iced tea; iced tea spiced with cinnamon and cloves; iced tea mixed half-and-half with lemonade or cranberry juice; iced herbal or mint tea

• Yogurt smoothie (plain or vanilla yogurt blended with fresh fruit); flavored milk over ice; ice cream sodas; milk shakes

CHILLED CORN SOUP

Makes 5 cups

This soup takes advantage of the wonderful fresh corn found only in summer (although you certainly may make it with frozen corn, too, and even serve it hot in autumn and winter). A snap to make, and it can be prepared ahead with excellent results.

Note: This is an ample menu, so about ¾ cup of soup per person is plenty as a starter.

2 tablespoons butter or margarine
1 cup chopped red or yellow onion
   (about 1 medium onion)
½ red pepper, diced
1½ cups corn kernels, cut from
   2 fresh or frozen ears
Salt
Fresh pepper
2½ cups chicken broth
1 cup milk
2 tablespoons flour
1 teaspoon sugar (optional)

1. In a large saucepan, melt the butter or margarine and sauté the onion and pepper until soft. Add the corn and continue cooking for 3 minutes. Season with salt and pepper.

Meanwhile, heat the broth and milk in a small saucepan.

2. Add the flour to the corn mixture and cook, stirring, for 1 minute. Add the hot broth and milk and simmer until slightly thickened. Season with a little more salt and pepper if needed; if the corn was not very sweet, add the sugar.

Chill the soup and serve cold (but not icy).

• Lemonade or orangeade with fruit garnish or a squeeze of lime; fizzy fruit juice (juice concentrate mixed with seltzer—try grapefruit, apple or tangerine juice)

• Iced coffee; iced mocha (coffee enriched with a little evaporated milk and cocoa powder)

• White or red wine spritzer; white wine spritzer with a spoonful of Crème de Cassis (black currant liqueur); sangría (page 36); ice-cold champagne

CHICKEN MILANAISE

Makes enough for 6

Chicken Milanaise means boneless cutlets dipped first in egg white, then dredged in a cheese-flour-breadcrumb mixture and finally sautéed until crisp on the outside and tender on the inside.

Note: If you like an extra-crisp coating, try double-dredging. Simply double the amounts given for the egg white mixture and for the breading mixture (see step 2) and repeat the dipping and dredging process a second time before sautéing the cutlets.

4 whole boneless chicken breasts, skinned and halved

2 egg whites beaten lightly with 3 tablespoons water

10 tablespoons (½ cup plus 2 tablespoons) grated Parmesan cheese (2½ ounces)

10 tablespoons (½ cup plus 2 tablespoons) flour

10 tablespoons (½ cup plus 2 tablespoons) dry breadcrumbs

½ teaspoon paprika

1 teaspoon dried chervil, crumbled

½ teaspoon salt

Fresh pepper

3 tablespoons butter

3 tablespoons olive oil

1. Pull off the long, narrow pointed piece of chicken that is loosely attached to the underside of each breast half; remove the white tendon from each long piece. Pound the chicken (long pieces and breast halves) to ¼-inch thick. Set aside.

2. Pour the egg white mixture into a shallow dish. In a medium bowl, stir together the cheese, flour, breadcrumbs, paprika, chervil, salt and a good grinding of pepper; transfer this breading mixture to a piece of wax paper.

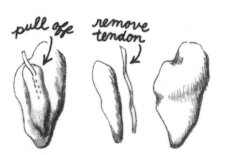

3. Dip 1 piece of chicken in the egg white mixture and let any excess drip off. Now dredge it in the breading mixture, making sure the chicken is thoroughly coated. Set aside on wax paper. Repeat with remaining pieces of chicken.

Note: If you're double-dredging, repeat the dipping and dredging process now.

4. Melt 1 tablespoon each of the butter and olive oil in a large skillet over medium heat, and sauté a third of the chicken pieces until well browned on both sides. Drain on paper towels. Place the chicken in 1 layer on a large baking sheet or ovenproof platter and keep warm in a 300° oven.

Repeat the process with the remaining butter, oil and chicken in 2 more batches. (Depending on your skillet, you may need a little extra oil for the second and third batches.)

Serve hot.

Salad Extras

Make your leafy salads more interesting by tossing in one or more additional ingredients from the list below. If necessary, cut them in appropriate shapes before adding—slices, cubes, slivers, wedges, bite-size pieces, etc.

Artichoke hearts	Fennel	Italian peppers	Pickles
Asparagus	Green beans	Jícama	Potatoes
Avocado	Green peas	Mushrooms	Red, white and black radishes
Beets	Hearts of palm	Olives	Red onions
Bell peppers			Scallions
Broccoli florets			Snow pea pods
Capers			Sprouts (alfalfa, radish, etc.)
Carrots			Sugar snap peas
Cauliflower florets			Sweet corn
Celery			Tofu
Celery root			Tomatoes
Cucumbers			Water chestnuts
Daikon (Japanese radish)			Zucchini

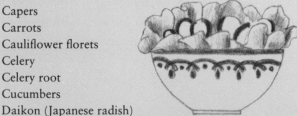

BABY GREEN BEANS
AND FRESH TOMATOES
WITH *SWEET-SOUR DRESSING*

Makes plenty for 6

Baby green beans are small, smooth and tender, with a wonderful flavor. However, they usually must be picked, one by one, out of a bin of large, tough, overgrown beans. This takes a little time and effort but do it if you possibly can.

3 medium-size ripe tomatoes
1½–2 pounds baby green beans,
　　stem ends trimmed

Sweet-Sour Dressing (recipe
　　follows)
Minced flat-leaf (Italian) parsley for
　　garnish

1. Core (remove the stem ends from) the tomatoes and cut in ⅛-inch slices. Arrange the slices, overlapping, around the edge of a serving platter.

2. In a large pot of boiling water, blanch the baby beans for 1 minute (large beans for 3 minutes). Drain, rinse briefly with cool water and drain again. Pat dry on paper towels, then place in a large bowl.

3. Pour about half the dressing on the warm beans and toss well. Arrange the beans attractively in the center of the platter. Drizzle the remaining dressing on the tomatoes and sprinkle with minced parsley. Serve warm or at room temperature.

SWEET-SOUR DRESSING
Makes about ½ cup

3 tablespoons red wine vinegar
1½ tablespoons water
¼ cup olive oil
1½ tablespoons tomato paste
¼ teaspoon dry mustard
1½ teaspoons sugar
¼ teaspoon salt

In a food processor or by hand, blend the ingredients until they are thoroughly amalgamated.

OVEN-BAKED PECAN WILD RICE

Makes about 4½ cups

A simple but delicious dish to bake while you are preparing the other dishes in this menu (or any other menu). The toasted pecans give the wild rice additional flavor and texture.

1 cup raw wild rice
1 cup chicken broth
½ cup water
2 or 3 tablespoons butter
1 teaspoon salt

Fresh pepper
⅔ cup chopped toasted pecans (see page 23 for toasting instructions)

1. Preheat the oven to 350°. Grease a 1½-quart casserole or other ovenproof dish. Wash the rice in a strainer under cold running water.

2. Pour the broth and water into the casserole, add the rice and stir once. Cover securely with a lid or aluminum foil and bake for 30 minutes.

3. Remove the lid and stir in the butter, salt, a good grinding of pepper and the toasted pecans. Cover and bake for 45 more minutes, or until the rice is just chewy and the liquid is absorbed; do not overcook. If needed, season with more salt and pepper.

Serve immediately or set aside for up to 20 minutes. If you set the rice aside, be sure to tilt the lid slightly or loosen the foil so steam can escape; this prevents sogginess.

Summer Produce Buying Guide

If you are lucky enough to have access to locally grown fresh produce, look for many of these fruits and vegetables, keeping in mind that availability changes as the summer progresses:

Basil, dill and other herbs
Eggplant
Green beans
Kirby cucumbers
Peppers
Summer lettuce (Bibb, oak leaf, red and green leaf, etc.)

Summer squash (zucchini, pattypan, etc.)
Sweet corn
Tomatoes

Berries (blackberries, raspberries, blueberries, etc.)
Cantaloupe

Casaba melon
Crenshaw melon
Figs
Honeydew melon
Nectarines
Peaches
Plums
Watermelon

APRICOTS WITH RICOTTA CREAM

Makes 6 servings

A classy dessert with a stylish presentation, but one that is still easy to prepare. Pair it with Almond Crunch Cookies (page 68), Cinnamon Snaps (page 38) or your favorite bakery cookies.

6 tablespoons heavy cream
¾ cup ricotta cheese
3 tablespoons superfine sugar
7½ tablespoons orange-flavored liqueur

12 medium or 18 small ripe apricots, halved and pitted
Grated semisweet chocolate for garnish (optional)

1. In a large bowl, whip the heavy cream. In another bowl, without cleaning the beaters, beat the ricotta cheese with the sugar and 1½ tablespoons of the liqueur, until well blended. Fold the whipped cream into the ricotta mixture. Set aside.

2. Make 5 cuts in each apricot half (3 cuts if the halves are small) as shown in the drawing. Divide the apricots among 6 dessert plates, fanning out the segments.

Drizzle 1 tablespoon of liqueur over the apricots on each plate. Put a sixth of the ricotta cream in the center of each plate and, if you like, top with a sprinkling of grated chocolate.

Served chilled or at room temperature.

Chicken Sandwiches

There's hardly a better sandwich than leftover roasted chicken on a big roll. For variety, try one of these combinations, some plain, some fancy:

• Chicken, chive cream cheese and arugula on pumpernickel

• Chicken, chutney and Boston lettuce on white toast

• Chicken, chopped olives, Italian pickled salad, thin-sliced provolone, thin-sliced tomatoes and romaine lettuce on a long roll brushed with olive oil

• Chicken, sun-dried tomatoes and sliced cucumber on sourdough bread or roll

• Chicken, crumbled goat cheese, sliced mushrooms and spinach leaves dressed with vinaigrette, stuffed into pita bread

• Chicken, sliced pickled beets, thin-sliced red onion and lettuce with horseradish mayonnaise on rye bread

Summer Menu #6

Tomato-Zucchini Salad
Middle Eastern flat bread (soft lavash or shepherd's bread)

HERB AND SPICE CHICKEN BAKED IN FOIL

Couscous with Dates and Carrots

Fresh figs
Creamy cheese, crackers and more flat bread

If you don't want to heat up the kitchen during a hot summer evening, simply begin one day ahead, baking the Herb and Spice Chicken after dark, when the temperature has dropped, and refrigerating it (immediately) for the next day's dinner.

Tip: Your choices of creamy cheese to serve for dessert are many and varied—Camembert, Crema Danica, Mascarpone, Boursin, Petit-Suisse and Montrachet, to name a few.

NOTES ON THE MENU

Can't find Lebanese or Armenian flat bread? Substitute white or whole wheat pita bread, each one split open into two flat rounds, and warmed to improve the flavor. Can't find fresh figs? Substitute dried ones, but be sure the dried ones are soft and haven't turned to fig leather.

TOMATO-ZUCCHINI SALAD

Makes plenty for 6

A good recipe for using up your garden's abundant crop of tomatoes, zucchini and basil. The vegetables are married in a shallot dressing that is certain to perk up late-summer appetites. Don't make it too far ahead—it's a fresh salad, not a marinated one.

½ cup olive oil
1–1¼ pounds small or medium
    zucchini, trimmed and cut in
    ½-inch dice
¼ cup balsamic vinegar
2 tablespoons minced shallots
¼ cup (packed) chopped fresh basil

¼ cup (packed) chopped flat-leaf
    (Italian) parsley
½ teaspoon salt
Fresh pepper
1–1¼ pounds ripe tomatoes, cored
    and cut in ½-inch dice
12–18 medium-size lettuce leaves
    (Boston, green leaf or red leaf)

1. Heat ¼ cup of the olive oil in a skillet over medium heat. Add the zucchini and cook, stirring, until the zucchini is crisp-tender. Set aside to cool.

2. In a large bowl, stir together the remaining olive oil, the vinegar, shallots, basil, parsley, salt and a good grinding of pepper. Stir in the tomatoes, then add the zucchini and olive oil from the skillet and mix well. Season with more salt and pepper if needed.

Serve mounded on individual salad plates lined with 2 or 3 lettuce leaves, with plenty of warm Middle Eastern bread on the side.

Lunch on the Patio

It's full summer—the season for inviting a few friends to lounge on the patio, to fan and chat and munch a light meal. Serve tall, cool drinks with this make-ahead cold lunch and don't plan to move anything but your mouths for at least three hours.

Cold Oven-fried Chicken Wings (page 18)
Chinese Cabbage Salad (page 50)
Cornbread or corn muffins

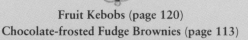

Fruit Kebobs (page 120)
Chocolate-frosted Fudge Brownies (page 113)

HERB AND SPICE CHICKEN BAKED IN FOIL

Makes plenty for 6

You won't believe how easy this is to make—or how moist and juicy the chicken will be when sealed and baked in foil. It's great-tasting at room temperature or cold and it's just as good served hot (in winter, if you like). And there's no pan to wash, either—a blessing in any weather.

1 tablespoon ground cumin
1 teaspoon cayenne pepper
1 teaspoon powdered dried thyme
1 tablespoon powdered dried oregano
1½ teaspoons salt

3 tablespoons flour
3 cloves garlic, very finely minced (about 1 heaping tablespoon)
9–11 whole chicken legs (thigh and drumstick)

1. Preheat the oven to 400°. Have ready a large roasting pan (no rack). Tear off 4 pieces of aluminum foil, each twice the length of the roasting pan. Take 2 pieces of the foil and pinch or fold them securely together along the long edges, as shown in the drawing, to make 1 large piece; repeat with the remaining pair of pieces. Place 1 large piece on top of the other and use the foil to line the roasting pan.

2. Stir together all the ingredients except the chicken. Arrange the chicken, skin side up, in 1 layer on a piece of wax paper. Sprinkle with half the herb and spice mixture, patting it on to make it adhere. Turn the chicken over and repeat with the remaining herb and spice mixture. Reserve all the herbs and spices that fall onto the wax paper.

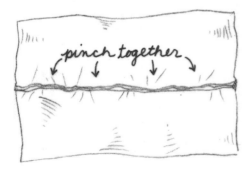

3. Arrange the chicken on the aluminum foil in the roasting pan. Sprinkle with the reserved herbs and spices. Bring the foil up and over the chicken to cover it completely. Pinch or fold the foil securely closed on the top and sides to seal the chicken in a foil package.

4. Bake for 1½ hours. Open the foil package carefully, to avoid being burned by the escaping steam. Use tongs to lift out the chicken and arrange it on a serving platter.

Serve the chicken warm or cool in summer, hot in winter.

Note: The liquid remaining in the foil-lined pan may be poured into a saucepan, skimmed and reduced, then served as a hot or cold sauce.

COUSCOUS WITH DATES AND CARROTS

Makes 6 cups

Making couscous is a cinch, even with extra ingredients added. This variation is slightly sweet and delicate, a mild companion to the more aggressively flavored chicken on the menu.

4 tablespoons (½ stick) butter
½ cup chopped onion (about 1 small onion)
1½ cups chicken broth
1½ cups water
¾ cup diced carrots (about 1½ medium carrots, trimmed and peeled)
1½ cups raw couscous
¾ cup pitted dates, chopped
Salt to taste

1. Melt the butter in a large skillet. Add the onion and sauté until soft.

2. Add the broth and water and bring to a boil. Add the carrots and simmer until the carrots are crisp-tender.

3. Stir in the couscous, making sure there are no lumps. Turn off the heat, cover the skillet and let stand 5 minutes, or until the couscous is soft and thoroughly cooked. If the liquid is absorbed and the couscous is still a little hard after 5 minutes, add ½ cup boiling water or broth, cover again and allow to stand for a few more minutes.

4. Add the dates (and salt if needed), and stir gently but thoroughly to distribute the bits. Serve hot or warm.

CHAPTER 4

CHICKEN DINNERS FOR AUTUMN AND WINTER

Menu #1
CHICKEN CUTLETS PUTTANESCA ON PAPPARDELLE

Menu #2
CHICKEN QUENELLES IN ESCAROLE SOUP

Menu #3
ROASTED CHICKEN WITH TART ORANGE SAUCE

Menu #4
CHICKEN POTPIE WITH BISCUIT TOPPING

Menu #5
CHICKEN STIR-FRY ON CRISP NOODLE CAKES

Menu #6
CHICKEN BRAISED WITH CIDER AND APPLES

Menu #7
CHICKEN WITH CREAM SAUCE AND PARSLEY DUMPLINGS

Menu #8
SIMPLE SKILLET CHICKEN WITH LEMON AND THYME

Menu #9
CHICKEN CURRY WITH CONDIMENTS

Menu #10
CHICKEN WITH SOUR CREAM
AND CORIANDER SAUCE

Menu #11
CHICKEN BREASTS STUFFED
WITH SAUSAGE AND PINE NUTS

Menu #12
MIDDLE EASTERN YOGURT-BAKED CHICKEN LEGS

When it's cold outside, there's nothing better than cozying up to a hot chicken dinner with family and friends. You'll notice right away that the menus in this chapter are substantial ones, featuring chicken recipes with good strong flavors, no-nonsense side dishes (lentils, chick peas, bread stuffings, fritters, etc.) and hearty desserts.

Fall and winter bring their own delicious seasonal produce—grapes and citrus fruits, a dozen varieties of apples and pears, sweet parsnips and beets, pungent leeks, dark green broccoli, kale and collards. You'll find many of these in the menus, too.

Note: On the menus, some of the dishes are listed in *italics*. No recipes are given for these basic or storebought items.

Autumn and Winter Menu #1

Baked Stuffed Mushrooms

CHICKEN CUTLETS PUTTANESCA ON PAPPARDELLE

Pan-browned Zucchini with Garlic
Italian bread

Brandied Fruit Compote
Amaretti or other Italian-style cookies

A rich, satisfying company or Sunday dinner. Much can be done ahead, if you like, including the chicken dish (but not the pasta, of course). To me, this meal is warmth and hospitality on a plate.

NOTES ON THE MENU

To streamline the menu for a weekday family dinner, omit the stuffed mushrooms and, instead of compote for dessert, serve amaretti or cookies with a pretty bowl of tangerines, pears or apples.

Autumn Produce Buying Guide

By September the bright colors of summer produce are giving way to the deeper colors and heartier textures of autumn produce. Here are some fruits and vegetables you'll start to see now, as well as a few that are available year-round but are especially satisfying in colder weather.

Beets	Leeks	Turnips	Apples
Broccoli	Mushrooms	Winter squash (acorn,	Cranberries
Brussels sprouts	Pumpkins	buttercup, butternut, delicata,	Grapes
Carrots	Rutabagas	dumpling, etc.)	Pears
Cauliflower	Sweet potatoes	Zucchini	Pomegranates
Chinese cabbage			
Collards			

BAKED STUFFED MUSHROOMS

Makes 6 servings

Try this technique for hollowing out a mushroom cap: First cut out the entire stem with the tip of a sharp paring knife. Next, carefully use a melon-baller to scoop some of the flesh from each cap—not too much, or the cap will split or break. Practice on one or two extra mushrooms to get the hang of it.

Another tip: Make the cracker crumbs in your food processor.

18 large white mushrooms
½ cup cracker crumbs
¼ cup grated Parmesan cheese
2 tablespoons minced flat-leaf (Italian) parsley

4 tablespoons (½ stick) soft butter
¼ cup white wine
1 teaspoon salt

1. Preheat the oven to 350°.

Hollow out the mushrooms as described in the introduction, reserving the stems and scooped-out flesh; set the mushroom caps aside in a buttered baking dish.

2. Put the mushroom stems and flesh in the bowl of a food processor with the remaining ingredients and process just until the stems are chopped fine. Do not overprocess.

3. Fill each mushroom cap with stuffing mixture, mounding it neatly in the center. Bake for 45 minutes and serve hot.

CHICKEN CUTLETS PUTTANESCA ON PAPPARDELLE

Makes plenty for 6

A robust, intensely flavored dish, ideal for a chilly night. Happily, the chicken can be prepared early in the day and refrigerated until needed (see step 6).

Note: The anchovies dissolve completely in the sauce; even anchovy-haters won't know they're there.

3 whole boneless chicken breasts, skinned and halved
Olive oil and butter for sautéing
1 cup chopped onion (about 1 medium onion)
6 cloves garlic, minced
2 pounds fresh plum tomatoes (about 12 medium), peeled (see page 59)
12–16 big, juicy green olives
Note: I use Sicilian olives, which I buy in an Italian delicatessen or specialty store.
2 tablespoons capers

12 anchovy fillets, drained and chopped (one 2-ounce can flat or rolled anchovy fillets)
½ cup red wine
¼ cup balsamic vinegar
½ cup water
Fresh pepper
Salt
1 pound fresh pappardelle or tagliatelle (¾- or ¼-inch-wide pasta)
Note: If you can't find either of these, use dried penne, mafalde, cut ziti, even linguine—any pasta that has bite.

1. Pull off the long, narrow pointed piece of chicken that is loosely attached to the underside of each breast half; remove the white tendon from each long piece. Pound the chicken (long pieces and breast halves) ¼ inch thick. Set aside.

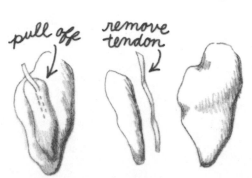

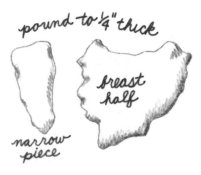

2. In a large heavy skillet, heat 2 tablespoons each of olive oil and butter. Sauté the chicken pieces in batches, until browned on both sides, adding a bit more oil and butter if needed. Set aside. Do not clean out the skillet.

3. In the same skillet, sauté the onions and garlic until soft. Turn off the heat while you prepare the rest of the ingredients.

4. Core the tomatoes and chop in a ½-inch dice. Cut the olive flesh away from the pits; chop in ¼-inch bits. If the capers are large, chop in half.

5. Add the tomatoes, olive bits, capers, anchovies, wine, vinegar, water and a good grinding of pepper to the skillet and stir well. Simmer for 15 minutes, stirring often; the sauce will be chunky. If needed, add salt to taste.

6. Add the chicken pieces to the sauce, layering if necessary, making sure they are well moistened. Cover and simmer for 5 minutes. Transfer the chicken and sauce to an ovenproof dish.

If you are serving the chicken now, cover the dish loosely with foil and keep warm in the oven while you prepare the pappardelle.

Alternatively, if you're preparing the chicken ahead of time, cover the dish with foil and refrigerate until needed. Before serving, bring the chicken to room temperature, then warm it in a preheated 325° oven for 15 minutes while you prepare the pasta.

7. Cook the pasta in a large pot of salted or unsalted boiling water just until al dente (2–3 minutes for fresh, 7–10 minutes for dried). Drain immediately, return the pasta to the pot and toss with 1 or 2 tablespoons of olive oil.

Spread the cooked pasta on a platter and arrange the chicken cutlets and sauce on top. Serve hot.

Simple Garnishes

Cucumber, mayonnaise and dill sprigs

Endive, zucchini and diced pepper

Baby beans tied in a bundle

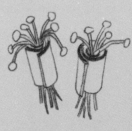

Cucumber curls and enoki mushrooms

PAN-BROWNED ZUCCHINI
WITH GARLIC

Makes about 4 cups

An uncomplicated but delicious treatment of this favorite squash. It is impossible to brown every piece of zucchini and still keep the dish from overcooking, so expect that only about half will be browned by the time the rest is properly cooked.

You may make the dish ahead and reheat it in a skillet.

6 medium or 8 small zucchini
   (about 2½ pounds)
Salt
1 tablespoon butter

2 tablespoons olive oil
4 cloves garlic, minced
Fresh pepper

1. Trim the zucchini and cut it in ¼-inch-thick rounds. Put the zucchini in a colander, sprinkle liberally with salt and toss to coat. Let the zucchini drain in the colander for 20 minutes, then rinse very well and drain again.

2. In a large skillet over low heat, melt the butter and olive oil, add the garlic and sauté for 1 minute.

3. Add the zucchini and sprinkle with a little salt and a good grinding of pepper. Sauté over high heat until tender and lightly browned, using a spatula to turn the zucchini frequently. Correct the seasoning, if necessary.

Serve immediately or refrigerate until 1 hour before serving time. Bring the dish to room temperature, then reheat quickly in the skillet.

BRANDIED FRUIT COMPOTE

Makes 5 cups

So much rich, sweet, pungent flavor for so little work. This particular combination of fruit is luscious, but you may use more or less of any fruit you choose, keeping the count roughly the same.

Tip: The compote tastes best if made a day ahead of time.

8 dried peaches
8 dried pears
8 large or 16 small dried apricots
8 dried figs, hard stem ends snipped off
8 pitted prunes
½ cup dark or light raisins

¼ cup sugar
¼ cup (packed) brown sugar
1 teaspoon grated lemon rind
3 tablespoons fresh lemon juice
1 cup brandy
½ cup water

1. Cut the peaches in half. Put the peaches, pears, apricots and figs in a large saucepan of cold water; bring to a boil and simmer, covered, for 20 minutes. Drain the fruit in a colander or strainer.

2. Return the cooked fruit to the saucepan. Add all the remaining ingredients, stir well and bring to a boil. Reduce the heat and simmer, uncovered, for 20 minutes, stirring often.

If you have made it a day ahead, refrigerate the compote until 1 hour before serving. If not, simply serve it warm or at room temperature. For an added treat, top each serving of compote with a dollop of ricotta cream (see page 80).

Holiday Food Presentation

Give some thought to the appearance of the meal you serve on your holiday table.

- Hors d'oeuvres and canapés should have finishing touches—a dab of mayonnaise sprinkled with paprika, a few capers and chopped onions, a slice of pimento-stuffed olive.
- Garnish soups with minced herbs, tiny dumplings or croutons, thin slices of cucumber, a swirl of cream.
- Salads may be edged with radish or tomato roses, sprigs of parsley or watercress, olives, finely shredded red cabbage, thin slices of apple, scallion flowers, carrot curls.

Autumn and Winter Menu #2

**Chicory Salad with Baked Goat Cheese and Roasted Red Pepper
Garlic Vinaigrette Sauce**
Crusty French bread or rolls

CHICKEN QUENELLES
IN ESCAROLE SOUP

Semolina Cake with Plum Sauce and Whipped Cream
Tangerines

An elegant Sunday supper, light but warming on a chilly night. Serve lots of bread and sweet butter with both the salad and soup.

NOTES ON THE MENU

To augment the dinner, serve guests an appetizer before the meal. Some possibilities: country pâté with cornichons; Wild Mushrooms on Toast (page 128); baked clams.

Also, expand the dessert selection to include grapes, lady apples, small pears, a bowl of walnuts in the shell.

- Serve bread and rolls in napkin-lined baskets or bowls, breadsticks in jars tied with ribbon.
- Garnish fish with lemon and lime wedges (or slices) sprinkled with minced parsley, finely diced colorful vegetables, capers, herbs, chopped nuts.
- Roasted chicken is festive when surrounded with baby vegetables, broiled mushroom caps, rosettes of mashed potato.
- Line plates of cookies or cake with paper doilies; decorate other desserts with slivers of orange rind, chocolate shavings, a sprinkling of toasted coconut.

CHICORY SALAD
WITH BAKED GOAT CHEESE
AND ROASTED RED PEPPER

Makes plenty for 6

This is quite a hearty, filling salad, which absolutely must have bread or rolls alongside. If convenient, prepare the various parts ahead and assemble the salad just before serving.

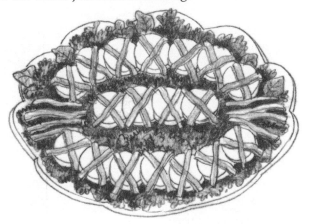

2 red bell peppers or one 7-ounce jar roasted red peppers
9-inch log of fresh goat cheese or equivalent in shorter logs, 2 inches in diameter
Olive oil
¼ cup fine dry breadcrumbs seasoned with freshly ground pepper

4 cups (packed) bite-size pieces of chicory (tender inner leaves are best)
3 cups (packed) sliced Belgian endive
3 cups (packed) bite-size pieces of arugula
Garlic Vinaigrette Sauce (recipe follows)
Salt
Fresh pepper

1. Preheat the oven to 400°.

Roast and peel the fresh red peppers (see page 54); remove the seeds and veins and cut the flesh in ⅛-inch strips. Pat the strips dry on paper towels.

If you are using peppers from a jar, rinse them and pat dry on paper towels; remove seeds and veins and cut the flesh in ⅛-inch strips.

2. Cut 18 slices of cheese, each ½ inch thick, and lay them on wax paper. Brush all over with olive oil and sprinkle breadcrumbs on all sides. Arrange the slices on a lightly oiled baking sheet and bake for 8 minutes. Carefully turn the slices with a spatula and bake for 4 more minutes. Let cool on the baking sheet.

3. Put the greens in a large bowl, dress with Garlic Vinaigrette Sauce to taste, and toss well. Correct the seasoning with salt and pepper if necessary.

4. Arrange the dressed greens on a large serving platter. Top with the slices of baked cheese and the strips of red pepper. Serve immediately.

GARLIC VINAIGRETTE SAUCE
Makes about 1 cup

¼ cup balsamic or red wine vinegar
¾ cup olive oil or combination of
    olive and other vegetable oil
¼ teaspoon salt

½ teaspoon dry mustard
Fresh pepper to taste
1 clove garlic, split in half

1. In a food processor or by hand, blend all ingredients except the garlic until thoroughly combined. Adjust the seasonings, if necessary, and pour into a jar with the garlic.

2. Let the dressing stand at room temperature for about 2 hours to develop a gentle garlic flavor. After that time, either remove the garlic or leave it in for a stronger kick. Use the dressing immediately or refrigerate until needed. Shake before using.

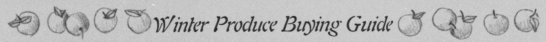

Winter Produce Buying Guide

Most kinds of produce that were available in autumn are still available in winter. It's the time of year when you must use all your ingenuity to keep your family eating fresh fruits and vegetables. In addition to the ones on page 87, here are some possibilities:

Artichokes	Fennel	Spinach	Grapefruit
Cabbage	Kale	Winter lettuce (Belgian endive,	Oranges
Celery root	Mushrooms	chicory, escarole, radicchio,	Tangerines
Chestnuts	Parsnips	romaine)	

CHICKEN QUENELLES
IN ESCAROLE SOUP

Makes plenty for 6

Chicken quenelles are light little poultry dumplings poached in broth. Using a food processor shortens the dumpling preparation significantly.

For the quenelles
2 cups diced boneless, skinless raw chicken breast (a little more than 1 pound)
6 tablespoons butter, melted
2 eggs
¼ cup heavy cream

1 teaspoon salt
2 pinches nutmeg

For the soup
1 head escarole
8 cups chicken broth
⅓ cup water

1. Put all the ingredients for the quenelles in a food processor or blender and process (in batches if necessary) until completely smooth. Refrigerate until chilled.

2. Meanwhile, cut the stem end off the escarole and discard the tough outer leaves. Wash and dry the remaining leaves, and cut them into enough bite-size pieces to make 4 packed cups. Set aside.

3. When the chicken mixture is cold, bring the broth to a boil in a stockpot or large skillet. Drop neat teaspoons (regular teaspoons, not measuring spoons) of chicken mixture into the boiling broth, using up half the mixture. Cook, uncovered, for 7 minutes, keeping the broth at a low boil, stirring often. Use a slotted spoon to remove the quenelles. Repeat with the remaining chicken mixture.

4. Lower the heat under the broth, add the water and the escarole and simmer for 10 minutes. Add the quenelles, stir well and ladle the hot soup into a tureen or individual bowls.

SEMOLINA CAKE WITH PLUM SAUCE AND WHIPPED CREAM

Makes 1 loaf cake

This lovely cake is leavened with egg whites and has a delicately crunchy texture, thanks to the semolina flour and ground almonds. Since it is so delicate, it's best to make and eat the cake on the same day or make it ahead and freeze it, snugly wrapped in plastic.

Note: Buy semolina flour in a gourmet shop or health food store.

6 eggs, yolks and whites separated into two large deep bowls
1 cup sugar
Grated rind and juice of 1 medium lemon (about 1½ teaspoons rind, 4 teaspoons juice)
1 teaspoon vanilla extract

1 cup semolina flour
Pinch of salt
¾ cup ground almonds (about ¾ cup whole unblanched almonds)
Plum Sauce (recipe follows)
Slightly sweetened whipped cream

1. Preheat the oven to 350°. Grease and flour a 9½ × 5½ × 2¾-inch loaf pan.

In a large bowl, beat the egg yolks and sugar until pale and very thick, about 5 minutes at medium speed. Add the grated rind, lemon juice and vanilla and blend well. Add the semolina flour and salt and beat at low speed. Add the ground almonds and blend well *by hand;* the mixture will be very thick. Set aside.

2. With clean, dry beaters, beat the egg whites until they hold firm, glossy, moist peaks. Fold a third of the whites into the stiff batter to lighten it, then fold the rest of the egg whites into the lightened batter. Immediately pour the batter into the prepared pan.

3. Bake for 45–50 minutes, or until a cake tester inserted in the center of the cake comes out clean. The cake will be firm and golden. Let it cool for 15 minutes in the pan on a wire rack, then turn out to finish cooling, right side up, on the rack. Serve in slices, each slice drizzled with 2 tablespoons of Plum Sauce and topped with slightly sweetened whipped cream.

PLUM SAUCE
Makes about ¾ cup

1¾ cups canned whole purple
    plums in syrup (one 1-pound
    can)

1 tablespoon sugar
2 tablespoons port wine
3 slices lemon, seeds removed

1. Strain the syrup from the can of plums into the bowl of a food processor. Remove the pits from the plums and add the pitted plums to the bowl. (Be very careful to remove every pit or you'll destroy your processor.) Process until almost smooth.

2. Put the plum purée and the remaining ingredients in a saucepan over low heat and cook, uncovered, stirring occasionally, until reduced to a scant cup. Remove the lemon slices and let the sauce cool. Store in the refrigerator.

Chicken Sandwich Suppers

Leftover chicken is great for sandwiches (see page 80), and chicken sandwiches are great starting points for light, filling meals that require little cooking. Simply add soup, salad, side dish and/or dessert to turn chicken sandwiches into supper.

- **Soups:** cream of celery; lentil; vegetable; corn chowder; tomato; vegetable minestrone topped with Parmesan cheese; French onion; black bean; cream of mushroom; borscht

- **Salads:** tossed green; cucumber; avocado vinaigrette on lettuce; spinach; Waldorf; three bean; mushroom; tomato

- **Side dishes:** coleslaw; potato salad; baked beans; pasta salad; asparagus or green beans vinaigrette; marinated artichoke hearts; roasted peppers; olives, pickles and other condiments; chutney; applesauce; crudités

- **Desserts:** cookies of all kinds; banana, date-nut or other loaf cake; pound cake; gingerbread; cupcakes; pudding; fruit tarts; fruit salad; whole fresh fruit; baked or stewed fruit

Autumn and Winter Menu #3

Three Stuffed Vegetables

ROASTED CHICKEN
WITH TART ORANGE SAUCE

Sherried Chestnut Stuffing
Braised Leeks
Cranberry Chutney
Dinner rolls

Apple-Raisin Pie with Sour Cream Pastry
Cheddar cheese

This deluxe dinner is suitable for Thanksgiving, Christmas or any other major occasion, especially if you're ready for a change from the usual turkey-and-creamed-onion menu.

NOTES ON THE MENU

There are a lot of ways to build this menu into a holiday extravaganza, particularly if several cooks get in on the act.

For instance, add Lima Beans in Onion Sauce (page 132) or Baked Brussels Sprouts (page 137). Serve baked sweet potatoes or Corn Fritters (page 136). More desserts are always welcome, too—Christmas cookies, fruitcake, pumpkin pie, trifle, a beautiful platter of cut fruit.

THREE STUFFED VEGETABLES

Each recipe makes 3 or 4 pieces for 6

Since each short recipe yields only several pieces per person, make two or three of the recipes or double any one of them when you want to provide a substantial hors d'oeuvre.

CHERRY TOMATOES
WITH SMOKED MUSSELS

18 cherry tomatoes
¼ cup sour cream, stirred smooth in a small bowl

18 smoked mussels, rinsed and drained on paper towels (one 3½-ounce can)
Hot English or Chinese prepared mustard

1. Slice off the bottom (not the stem end) of each cherry tomato and use a small melon baller to scoop out and discard the juice and seeds.

2. Smear a heaping half teaspoon of sour cream on 1 end of each mussel and stuff that end into a hollow tomato. Put a dab of mustard on the tip of each mussel.

ZUCCHINI WITH ROASTED GARLIC

2 slender zucchini, each about
    7 inches long, trimmed
25 *unpeeled* cloves garlic, roasted
    for 20 minutes in a small pan in
    a preheated 375° oven

1 tablespoon mayonnaise
Salt
Fresh pepper
Capers, sun-dried tomatoes or
    roasted peppers for garnish

1. Cut the zucchini in ½-inch slices; use a melon baller to scoop flesh out of each slice, leaving ¼ inch at the bottom and sides.

2. Peel the roasted garlic and cut off the hard stem ends. Purée or thoroughly mash the soft flesh with the mayonnaise and season with salt and pepper.

3. Put a small spoonful of the garlic mixture in each scooped-out slice of zucchini and garnish with a couple of capers, a snippet of sun-dried tomato or a tiny strip of pepper.

scoop out

CELERY WITH HERB CHEESE

Small log of herbed goat cheese
Cream or half-and-half

6 or more stalks celery, trimmed
Fresh pepper

1. Mash the goat cheese with 1 or 2 tablespoons of cream, to make the cheese spreadable.

2. Use a small spatula to stuff and mound the cheese in the centers of the celery stalks. Cut in 1½-inch pieces and sprinkle with pepper.

ROASTED CHICKEN
WITH TART ORANGE SAUCE

Makes plenty for 6

This is basic roasted chicken with a citrus twist: The lemons give it a subtle infusion of flavor while it roasts and the tart sauce brightens it when it is served.

2 chickens, about 3½ pounds each
Salt
Fresh pepper
5 lemons, room temperature
2 juice oranges, room temperature

1 cup chicken broth
¼ cup Grand Marnier
1 teaspoon sugar
4 navel oranges

1. Preheat the oven to 375°.

Salt and pepper the chickens, inside and out. Take 4 of the lemons and pierce them all over with a kitchen fork; stuff 2 lemons in the cavity of each chicken. Tie the legs together loosely at the ankles. (This is a strictly esthetic provision; trussing keeps the chicken legs from splaying during roasting, making a neater presentation at table.)

Place the chickens, breast up, side by side on a rack in a roasting pan and roast for 1½ hours (or 2 hours, if you prefer the chicken well done).

2. Meanwhile, squeeze the juice from the remaining lemon and the 2 juice oranges and put it in a saucepan with the chicken broth, Grand Marnier and sugar. Simmer briskly until reduced by a third, about 20 minutes.

Meanwhile, cut the skin and white pith from the navel oranges; cut the oranges in ¼-inch slices.

3. When the chickens are done, remove the string and discard the lemons. Pierce the skin near the thighs and let the juices run out into the roasting pan. Transfer the chickens to an ovenproof platter and keep them warm in a low oven.

4. Remove the rack from the roasting pan. Skim the fat from the juice in the roasting pan, then pour the juice into the reduced sauce in the saucepan. Simmer until reduced again.

Pour half the sauce over the 2 chickens. Place 3 overlapping slices of orange on each chicken for garnish and arrange the remaining orange slices around the edge of the platter.

Carve and serve at the table, passing the remaining sauce in a sauceboat.

SHERRIED CHESTNUT STUFFING

Makes about 5 cups

The combination of sherry, chestnuts and cream is irresistible in this breadcrumb stuffing.

Depending on how much patience and cash you have, make the dish with either fresh chestnuts, shelled, peeled and boiled (tedious but economical); whole peeled cooked chestnuts from a jar (easy but expensive); or reconstituted and boiled dried chestnuts (the middle ground). Please note that the stuffing is baked in the oven, not in the bird. It tastes better cooked that way.

3 cups coarsely chopped cooked
   chestnuts
5 cups soft white breadcrumbs,
   crusts removed first (about
   15 ounces of premium sliced
   white bread with crusts)
   Note: Use slightly stale bread; to
   make breadcrumbs, remove the
   crusts and tear bread into small
   bits or large crumbs.

¼ cup (packed) minced flat-leaf
   (Italian) parsley
1 teaspoon salt
Fresh pepper
8 tablespoons (1 stick) butter
½ cup cream sherry
½ cup cream or half-and-half

1. Butter a 1½-quart baking dish. Preheat the oven to 375° (350° for ovenproof glass).

In a large bowl, stir together the chestnuts, breadcrumbs, parsley, salt and a grinding of pepper.

2. Melt the butter with the sherry and cream, stirring to blend. Pour the butter mixture over the chestnut mixture and toss well. Pack the stuffing lightly into the buttered baking dish and bake, uncovered, for 45 minutes.

Note: The stuffing may be baked along with the roasted chicken, in which case you should put it in the oven 45 minutes before the chicken would be done.

BRAISED LEEKS

Makes enough for 6

You get a lot of flavor for very little work and very few ingredients here. This is a delicious dish for spring as well as fall, since peak availability of leeks is from October through May.

12–15 slim leeks, root ends and green parts cut off	Salt
3 tablespoons butter	Fresh pepper
Chicken or vegetable broth	2 teaspoons Dijon-style prepared mustard

1. Cut each leek in half lengthwise and wash thoroughly under cold running water, spreading the layers apart to remove sand and dirt. Pat dry on paper towels.

2. In a large skillet, melt the butter, add the leeks (in batches if necessary) and brown over low heat for 5 minutes, turning once. With all the leeks in the skillet, add enough broth to fill the skillet with ½ inch of liquid. Season with a little salt and pepper. Cover the skillet and cook the leeks over low heat for about 10 more minutes or until tender.

(At this point, you may uncover the skillet and set the leeks aside until serving time. If you do, be sure to cover and warm them briefly in the skillet before proceeding to step 3.)

3. Transfer the leeks to an ovenproof platter and keep warm in a low oven. Simmer the liquid in the skillet until reduced by half. Stir in the mustard and pour the sauce over the leeks. Serve hot.

Quick and Easy Thanksgiving Centerpieces

Tradition is the thing at Thanksgiving, so create your centerpiece from time-honored components—fruit, fall flowers, American pottery and so on—in rich autumn colors such as red, rust, brown, gold, teal, deep green. You'll want unscented candles on the table, too—short ones in votive glasses, tall ones in pewter holders or perhaps small hurricane lamps.

- Arrange dried flowers and grasses in small stoneware crocks; group the crocks on colorful straw mats. Baskets, Shaker boxes and toleware work beautifully, too.

CRANBERRY CHUTNEY

Makes about 3 cups

Tangy and spicy, with a bit of crunch from the walnuts and mellow sweetness from the dates—a perfect accompaniment to chicken, as well as turkey, pork roast, or ham. Good on chicken sandwiches, too.

1 pound cranberries, rinsed and drained

1 Granny Smith apple, peeled, quartered, cored and chopped in ¼-inch dice
Note: Be sure to remove all the seeds and hard matter when coring the apple.

½ cup chopped pitted dates

½ cup chopped toasted walnuts (see page 23 for toasting instructions)

¾ cup chopped onion (about 1 medium onion)

2 cloves garlic, minced

½–1 teaspoon minced ginger

1 cup sugar

½ cup cider vinegar

½ teaspoon cinnamon

¼ teaspoon ground cloves

¼ teaspoon ground allspice

⅛ teaspoon salt

1. Combine all the ingredients in a large, nonreactive saucepan (stainless steel, enameled, etc.). Bring slowly to a boil, stirring to dissolve the sugar.

2. Turn the heat down very low and simmer, uncovered, for 30–35 minutes, stirring often to prevent burning.

Let the chutney cool; it will thicken even more as it cools. If it is too thick for your taste, add a little water.

- Fill a group of pretty ceramic pitchers with branches of bittersweet and firethorn; add foliage and a few yellow chrysanthemums.
- Nest a duck decoy (or other carved wooden birds) in a large flat basket filled with dried grasses, cattails and seed pods.
- Well-polished copper molds can be piled with nuts and small fruits such as kumquats, clementines, lady apples and Seckel pears.
- A cornucopia basket overflowing with apples, pears, tangerines, pomegranates, grapes and unshelled nuts is always a perfect Thanksgiving centerpiece.

APPLE-RAISIN PIE
WITH SOUR CREAM PASTRY

Makes one 9-inch, double-crust pie

Here's a scrumptious, lattice-topped apple pie, worthy of any festive occasion. The filling does have more ingredients than you might expect, but it is not a bit difficult to make and the pie dough is singularly easy to handle.

Nine-inch metal pie pans seem to be scarce these days, so you'll probably be using a glass pie pan. In either case, the pan should measure nine inches across the top (inner edge to inner edge) and about 1½ inches high.

For the pie dough

8 tablespoons (1 stick) cold margarine, cut in small chunks
3 tablespoons cold butter, cut in small chunks
2 cups flour stirred with a pinch of salt and 1 tablespoon sugar
¾ cup sour cream

For the pie filling

2¼–2½ pounds firm tart apples (such as Granny Smith, Stayman, Northern Spy, Jonathan or Rhode Island Greening), peeled, quartered and cored
Note: Be sure to remove all the seeds and hard matter.

½ cup light or dark raisins
Grated rind of ½ lemon
2 teaspoons fresh lemon juice
3 tablespoons butter, melted and cooled
½ teaspoon vanilla extract
9 tablespoons sugar
2 tablespoons flour
½ teaspoon cinnamon
Pinch of salt
¼ cup apple or cranberry juice
1 tablespoon flour mixed with 1 tablespoon sugar
3 tablespoons half-and-half or a combination of milk and heavy cream

Half-and-half, milk or cream and sugar for glazing the crust

1. Make the pie dough: Cut the margarine and butter into the flour mixture until the mixture first resembles breadcrumbs and then begins to clump. Dot with all but 1 tablespoon of the sour cream and mix with a fork; the mixture will be quite sticky. With your fingers, work the dough just until you can form a ball that holds together firmly; if necessary, add the reserved tablespoon of sour cream.

2. Divide the dough in 2 pieces, one slightly larger than the other; wrap the smaller piece in plastic and set aside. Roll out the larger piece between pieces of plastic wrap or wax paper or on a well-floured board to make a bottom crust at least 13 inches in diameter.

3. Peel off the top piece of plastic wrap or wax paper and invert the dough into the pie pan, pressing it down firmly; peel away the second piece of plastic wrap or wax paper. If you rolled the dough on a floured board, gently fold it in half, center it on half of the pie pan and unfold. Trim excess dough to a 1-inch overhang and patch the crust if necessary. Set aside while you make the filling.

4. Make the pie filling: Cut the apples to make ¼-inch slices, as shown.

In a large bowl, mix the apples and all the remaining filling ingredients except the last two (the flour-sugar mixture and the half-and-half).

5. Preheat the oven to 425°.

Sprinkle the flour-sugar mixture on the bottom crust. Add the filling, mounding it slightly in the center. Drizzle the 3 tablespoons of half-and-half evenly over the filling.

6. Roll out the second piece of dough between pieces of plastic wrap or wax paper or on a well-floured board, to a rectangle about 12 inches long and ⅛ inch thick. Peel off the plastic wrap or wax paper and cut the dough lengthwise in ¾-inch-wide strips for a lattice top. Weave the strips over the filling, then trim excess dough and seal the strips to the bottom crust with a bit of water. Roll up the overhanging dough of the bottom crust and crimp it neatly.

Glaze the crust (both the lattice and the crimped edge) by brushing with half-and-half (or milk or cream) and sprinkling with a little sugar.

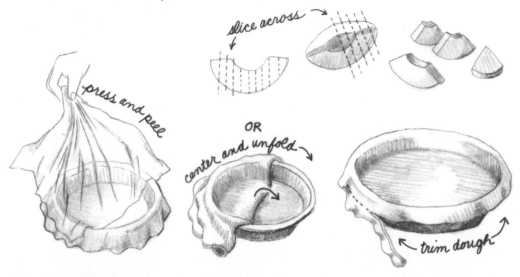

slice across

press and peel

OR

center and unfold

trim dough

7. Place the pie pan on the lowest shelf of the oven, with a piece of foil on the oven floor to catch the drips. Bake for 15 minutes at 425°, then reduce the temperature to 350° for a glass pie pan, 375° for a metal pan, and bake for 30–40 minutes more, or until the apples are crisp-tender and the crust is golden.

Note: Test the apples by piercing with the point of a knife. The apples should be firm but not resistant.

Serve hot, warm or at room temperature.

Autumn and Winter Menu #4

CHICKEN POTPIE
WITH BISCUIT TOPPING

Crunchy Vegetable Relish

Poached Pears
Chocolate-frosted Fudge Brownies

This is the perfect one-dish main course, in my opinion, with crunchy salad for contrast and a slightly wicked dessert.

Tip: No one ever has enough of the biscuit topping, so consider making an extra batch of hot Onion Biscuits (page 61) or Drop Biscuits (page 21) to serve with the potpie.

NOTES ON THE MENU

Should you forget to start the vegetable relish in time, you can serve a simple green salad alongside (literally—on salad plates) the potpie. And fresh pears instead of poached make a fine accompaniment to fudge brownies—so does coffee ice cream, for that matter.

When company's coming, precede the meal with a simple appetizer of caraway-seeded cheese and whole-grain crackers, with small bowls of radishes and olives. Garnish the mounded vegetable relish with halved cherry tomatoes and squares of green pepper.

CHICKEN POTPIE
WITH BISCUIT TOPPING

Makes plenty for 6

One of America's favorite foods, made in many different regional styles. In my version the biscuit topping is thin and crisp and there's plenty of gravy.

You will need a shallow 2½-quart (ten-cup) baking dish; I use a rectangular ovenproof glass baking dish.

Note: Use all white meat or a combination of white and dark meat.

3 cups chicken broth
1 cup dry white wine
3 cups ¾-inch cubes boneless, skinless raw chicken (about one 4-pound whole chicken or 1½ pounds boneless chicken breasts)
1½ cups ¼-inch cubes raw carrot (4–5 medium carrots)
1½ cups ½-inch cubes raw potato (2–3 medium potatoes)
1½ cups frozen petite peas
4 tablespoons butter
6 tablespoons flour

½ teaspoon powdered dried thyme
Salt
Fresh pepper
1 recipe dough for Onion Biscuits (page 61)
Note: Except for preheating the oven to 450°, follow steps 1 and 2 of the Onion Biscuits recipe to make the dough. Omit the last 2 ingredients (melted butter and Parmesan cheese). Steps 4 and 5 below tell you what to do with the dough.

1. Pour the chicken broth and wine into a large skillet and bring to a simmer. Add the chicken, carrots and potatoes, pressing them into an even layer. Cover the skillet and return to a simmer. Tilt the lid slightly so steam can escape and cook for 15 minutes.

Turn off the heat, add the peas, cover and leave the ingredients in the skillet for 15 more minutes. Strain the hot broth from the skillet into a bowl.

2. Preheat the oven to 375° for a glass baking dish, 400° for a metal or ceramic dish.

In a heavy medium saucepan, melt the butter over low heat. Add the flour and cook, stirring, for 1 minute. Add the hot broth from step 1 all at once and whisk briskly. Bring to a boil, lower the heat and stir until the sauce is smooth and thickened. Add the thyme, salt to taste and a good grinding of pepper.

3. Pour the sauce over the ingredients in the skillet and stir well. Taste again and correct seasoning if necessary. Transfer the mixture to a 2½-quart shallow baking dish and set aside.

4. On a flour-dusted surface, roll the biscuit dough ⅛–¼ inch thick and cut with a 2-inch biscuit or cookie cutter. Gather the excess dough, knead it together and roll it out again to cut more rounds, for a total of 32 rounds.

5. Arrange the biscuit rounds on the chicken mixture, overlapping slightly as shown in the drawing. If your baking dish is a different shape, adjust the arrangement of biscuit rounds to fit neatly.

6. Bake on the center shelf of the oven for 35–40 minutes, or until the biscuit topping is lightly browned and crisp. Serve hot.

Winter Vegetable Combinations

The carrot and parsnip purée on page 131 is a good example of hearty vegetables combined to appeal to winter-weary appetites. Be adventurous and try some others:

• Baked butternut squash, coarsely mashed with butter and a bit of grated lemon rind, garnished with a confetti of baby lima beans, diced red pepper and corn kernels

• Cooked cubed beets and cooked cubed potatoes, sautéed with onions, dressed with a little cream, salt and pepper

• Butter-browned slices of cauliflower with diced roasted red peppers, slivers of sun-dried tomato and a few hot pepper flakes

• Sliced, cooked sweet potatoes and carrots coarsely mashed with a little butter and cream, baked in a casserole with peeled, sliced raw apples until the apples are cooked

• Shredded cabbage and sliced onions browned in oil and dressed with caraway seeds and white wine vinegar

• Creamed spinach with raisins and chopped walnuts

• Broccoli stir-fried with garlic, water chestnuts and dried Chinese mushrooms that have been reconstituted in warm water

CRUNCHY VEGETABLE RELISH

Makes 4–5 cups

If you like, prepare the vegetables one day ahead, but do not mix them with the hot dressing. The relish must marinate for at least two hours, but not more than eight.

1½–2 cups of ½-inch cubes of trimmed, peeled and seeded cucumber
1 cup of ¼-inch cubes of celery
1½–2 cups of ½-inch squares of red cabbage
Note: If you like, use ½ cup white cabbage and 1–1½ cups red cabbage.
½ cup minced red onion

For the dressing
½ cup cider vinegar
¼ cup water
¼ cup sugar
¼ cup vegetable oil (not olive oil)
½ teaspoon salt
½ teaspoon dry mustard
1 teaspoon mustard seeds
¼ teaspoon celery seeds

Red leaf or romaine lettuce, torn in pieces

1. In a large bowl, stir together the cucumber, celery, cabbage and red onion. Set aside.

2. Make the dressing: Bring the vinegar, water and sugar to a boil in a small saucepan, stirring to dissolve the sugar. Turn off the heat, add the remaining dressing ingredients and whisk until blended.

3. Pour the hot dressing over the vegetables and stir well. Marinate at room temperature for at least 2 hours (but not more than 8 hours), stirring occasionally. Refrigerate until needed.

At serving time, use a slotted spoon to mound the vegetables on a bed of red leaf or romaine lettuce. Discard any dressing left over in the large bowl. Serve chilled or at room temperature.

POACHED PEARS

Makes 6 servings

These small pears, cooked gently in spiced wine syrup, can be made ahead and refrigerated, then brought to room temperature before serving. I've allowed three small pears per person, but if you think more are needed, increase the other ingredients proportionately.

Tip: Whole poached pears make a handsome and unusual garnish for roasted chicken, placed around the edge of the platter with sprigs of curly-leaf parsley between them.

18 small Seckel pears
2 cups water
1 cup robust red wine
½ cup sugar
2 three-inch strips orange zest

⅛ teaspoon cinnamon
⅛ teaspoon nutmeg
Strips of orange zest for garnish
   (optional)

1. Peel the pears, leaving the stems attached. Set aside.

2. In a large, nonreactive saucepan (stainless steel, enameled, etc.), bring the remaining ingredients to a boil and stir to dissolve the sugar. Turn off the heat and arrange the pears in 1 layer in the pan. Bring the liquid barely to a simmer and cook, uncovered, for 15–20 minutes, turning several times and spooning the poaching liquid over them often. The pears are done when they can be pierced easily with the point of a knife.

3. Remove the pears with a slotted spoon. Turn the heat up to medium and simmer the poaching liquid until it is reduced to a syrup, about 15 minutes.

4. Return the pears to the pan with the heat off. Stir and turn them gently to coat with hot syrup, then arrange the pears on a serving platter. Pour the remaining syrup over the pears. Garnish with additional narrow strips of orange zest, if desired.

CHOCOLATE-FROSTED FUDGE BROWNIES

Makes 16 squares or 18 bars

Moist, chewy brownies come from the center of the pan, crisper ones from the sides—something for every taste. A light chocolate frosting definitely gilds the lily, but chocolate-lovers don't seem to mind.

3 squares (3 ounces) unsweetened chocolate
6 tablespoons butter or margarine
1½ tablespoons light corn syrup
2 eggs
9 tablespoons sugar
½ cup (packed) light brown sugar
1 teaspoon vanilla extract

¾ cup flour stirred with a pinch of salt
¾ cup chopped toasted pecans or walnuts (optional; see page 23 for toasting instructions)
Chocolate Butter Frosting (recipe follows)

1. Preheat the oven to 350°; grease an 8-inch-square baking pan.

In a small saucepan over very low heat, melt the chocolate, butter (or margarine) and corn syrup, stirring constantly. Set aside to cool.

2. In a large bowl, beat the eggs. Gradually add the sugar and brown sugar, beating well after each addition, until pale tan and very thick. Add the vanilla and the cooled chocolate mixture and beat again. Add the flour and blend well at low speed. If you are using nuts, add them and stir well.

3. Pour the batter into the prepared pan and spread evenly. Bake for 30–35 minutes on the center shelf of the oven, or until a cake tester inserted in the center of the pan comes out moist and a tester inserted 1 inch from the side of the pan comes out dry. Let the brownies cool completely in the pan on a wire rack. Do not cut in squares or bars yet.

Carefully turn out the brownies onto another wire rack, then invert onto a serving platter. Spread the top with frosting. Cut in squares or bars just before serving.

CHOCOLATE BUTTER FROSTING
Makes about ⅔ cup

This recipe may be doubled with fine results.

1½ tablespoons butter, room
    temperature
¾ cup confectioner's sugar
¼ teaspoon vanilla extract

Pinch of salt
1 square (1 ounce) unsweetened
    chocolate, melted and cooled
4 teaspoons cream or half-and-half

1. In a medium bowl, cream the butter. Gradually add ¼ cup of the sugar, beating after each addition. Add the vanilla, salt and chocolate and beat again.

2. Gradually beat in the remaining ½ cup sugar alternately with the cream, until the frosting is smooth and spreadable.

If some time will elapse before use, press a piece of plastic wrap directly onto the frosting to prevent a crust from forming. Store in a cool place (not the refrigerator) until needed. If the frosting becomes too thick to spread easily, stir in a bit more cream.

Cold-Weather Salads 1

Cold-weather salads can be as refreshing as summer salads, but they should be a bit heartier and, of course, make use of autumn and winter vegetables. The combinations suggested on page 125 are delicious with your favorite vinaigrette dressing. And if you've never had salad with warm vinaigrette, try this: Whisk the vinaigrette until very well combined, pour into a small saucepan and heat gently until warm but not hot. Use for dressing tossed salad (the greens will wilt slightly—that's the idea) or pour the warm sauce over arranged salads and serve immediately.

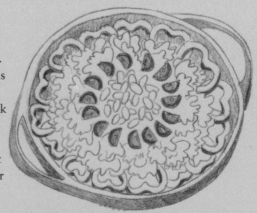

Autumn and Winter Menu #5

Cold Spiced Eggplant

CHICKEN STIR-FRY
ON CRISP NOODLE CAKES

Broccoli and Onions with Oyster Sauce

Fruit Kebobs
Vanilla ice cream with candied ginger

If you've never done stir-frying before, please note that stir-fry dishes (in this case, the chicken and the broccoli) require more preparation than they require actual cooking, so read the recipes carefully and have all the ingredients ready for the final, fast, stir-frying step. (The eggplant, the noodle cakes and the fruit—all non-stir-fry dishes—should be made ahead.)

NOTES ON THE MENU

If you can't manage the noodle cakes on a busy day, plain rice will do just fine here, too. It's a matter of available time. And speaking of time—when you're pressed for it, mandarin oranges (canned or fresh) are good for dessert, too, with or without the ice cream.

COLD SPICED EGGPLANT

Makes about 3½ cups

This is a soft, chunky spread with a rich flavor. The tricky part is what to serve it on. I like thin rice crackers, but plain crackers or crisp toasts are good, too.

Prepare the eggplant ahead since you'll be busy stir-frying later.

2 medium eggplants (about 1¾ pounds)
Salt
2 tablespoons white sesame seeds
3 tablespoons soy sauce
2 tablespoons rice vinegar
2 tablespoons sugar
2 tablespoons rice wine or dry sherry
¼ teaspoon hot red pepper flakes
2¼ cups water
2 tablespoons peanut oil
1½ tablespoons minced garlic
1½ tablespoons minced ginger
2 scallions, white and green parts, minced

1. Trim (but do not peel) the eggplants and cut into ¾-inch cubes. Place in a colander, sprinkle with salt, toss well and allow to drain for 30 minutes.

While the eggplant drains, toast the sesame seeds in a large skillet over low heat, shaking the pan to turn the seeds, just until the seeds are golden. Turn out onto a plate to cool.

Mix together the soy sauce, vinegar, sugar, wine (or sherry), pepper flakes and water; set aside.

2. Rinse the eggplant under cold running water. Squeeze gently, by the handful, to remove excess liquid. Heat the oil in the skillet used for toasting the sesame seeds, then add the eggplant, garlic and ginger, and sauté over high heat for 3 minutes.

3. Add the sauce mixture, bring to a simmer and stir well. Turn the heat down to medium low and simmer, uncovered, stirring occasionally, for 30 minutes or until the eggplant is tender and glazed and the liquid is gone.

Let the eggplant cool in the skillet. Add the minced scallions and toasted sesame seeds and stir well. Serve cold or at room temperature.

CHICKEN STIR-FRY
ON CRISP NOODLE CAKES

Makes enough for 6

A stir-fry like this one tastes best when the seasonings do not overwhelm the ingredients and when each one (in this case, chicken, dried mushrooms and snow pea pods) keeps its own distinctive flavor.

Note: To do a proper stir-fry, you must have all the ingredients prepared before you even heat the skillet or wok. And, of course, you'll have the Crisp Noodle Cakes ready and waiting.

2 teaspoons cornstarch
1 egg white
4 tablespoons dry sherry
1 pound boneless raw chicken breasts, skinned and then cut in slices ⅛ inch thick and no more than 3 inches long
12 Chinese dried mushrooms, soaked for 30 minutes in hot water

Crisp Noodle Cakes (recipe follows)
⅓ cup plus 1 tablespoon peanut oil
2 teaspoons minced garlic
2 teaspoons minced ginger
2 tablespoons soy sauce
¼ pound snow pea pods, trimmed

1. In a medium bowl, mix the cornstarch, egg white, and 2 tablespoons of dry sherry. Add the chicken slices and, using your fingers, mix well. Refrigerate for 30 minutes.

2. Drain the mushrooms and squeeze dry. Cut out and discard the stems; cut the remaining pieces of mushroom in narrow strips.

Put the noodle cakes in a 300° oven to warm.

3. Heat ⅓ cup of the peanut oil in a wok or large skillet; the oil should be very hot, almost smoking. Add the chicken and stir-fry until it turns white, about 2 minutes. Remove the chicken with a slotted spoon and drain on paper towels.

4. Add the remaining tablespoon of oil to the skillet. Add the garlic and ginger and stir-fry for about 15 seconds. Add the cooked chicken, the remaining 2 tablespoons of sherry, the soy sauce, snow pea pods and mushrooms and stir-fry for 2 minutes.

Mound half the chicken mixture on each noodle cake and serve immediately.

CRISP NOODLE CAKES
Makes 2 large cakes

1 pound dried thin Chinese or
Chinese-style egg noodles
*Note: If you can't find Chinese
egg noodles, use any thin egg
noodles. (Be sure you're buying
the right thing—most Italian
pasta is made without eggs.)*

2 tablespoons sesame oil
9 tablespoons peanut oil
6 scallions, green parts only,
minced (about ½ cup)
½ teaspoon salt

1. Cook the dried Chinese egg noodles for 3–5 minutes in a large pot of boiling water, just until al dente. (Other kinds of egg noodles may take longer.) Turn them into a colander and run cold water over them until they are cold. Help the noodles drain and dry by repeatedly lifting and separating them with your hands.

Turn the noodles into a large bowl, add the sesame oil, 1 tablespoon of the peanut oil, the scallions and salt and toss well with your hands. Divide in half into 2 bowls.

2. Heat 3 tablespoons of the remaining peanut oil in a 10–12-inch skillet over low-medium heat. When the oil is hot, add 1 bowl of the cold noodles, spreading them evenly in the pan. Press down with a spatula. Cook until the noodles on the bottom are golden brown, about 14 minutes. Be careful not to burn the noodles.

3. Turn the noodles: Using a spatula to help, slide the cake of noodles onto a baking sheet. Cover with a platter and invert. Add 1 tablespoon of peanut oil to the skillet and tilt the pan to coat it with oil. Slide the noodle cake back into the pan, cooked side up. Cook for 5–8 minutes, or until the bottom is golden brown.

Slide the noodles back onto the baking sheet or an ovenproof platter and set aside until ready to be reheated for the chicken stir-fry.

Repeat the process to make the second noodle cake.

BROCCOLI AND ONIONS WITH OYSTER SAUCE

Makes about 6 cups

You'll recognize the mellow taste of this sauce if you're accustomed to eating Chinese food. Be sure the blanched broccoli is crisp but tender, not overcooked.

For the sauce
3 tablespoons oyster sauce
   Note: Oyster sauce is available at Asian specialty stores, as well as some supermarkets.
1 cup chicken or vegetable broth
1 tablespoon cornstarch blended into 2 tablespoons dry sherry

6 cups broccoli florets or a combination of florets and peeled, sliced stems

2 tablespoons peanut oil
4 small yellow onions, sliced in wedges (as shown) and separated into individual pieces

1 tablespoon minced garlic

1. Make the sauce: In a saucepan, bring the oyster sauce and broth to a boil. Lower the heat, stir the cornstarch mixture again and add it to the saucepan. Simmer for 1 minute, stirring, until the sauce thickens. Set aside.

2. In a large pot of boiling water, blanch the broccoli for 3 minutes, just until crisp-tender. Drain, rinse under cold water and drain again, shaking off as much water as you can.

3. Heat the peanut oil in a wok or large skillet over high heat. Add the onions and stir-fry for several minutes, until lightly browned. Add the garlic and stir-fry for 10 seconds. Add the broccoli and stir-fry for 1 minute. Add the sauce and continue to stir for 1 more minute. Serve immediately.

FRUIT KEBOBS

Makes 18–24 kebobs

Fruit kebobs are bite-size pieces of fruit threaded on six-inch wooden skewers (the skewers are widely available at cookware and houseware stores, specialty food stores and some supermarkets). Kebobs make a delicious light dessert in any season: In summer, use attractively cut pieces of melon, peach, plum, nectarine and apricot; for fall and winter, choose any combination of the following fruits. Make three or four kebobs per person, with three or four pieces of fruit on each kebob.

- Navel oranges, peeled, quartered and sliced
- Seedless grapes
- Pineapple, peeled and cut in small cubes or wedges
- Red- or green-skinned apples, cored, sliced and cut in pieces
- Bananas, peeled and cut in thick slices
- Kiwi fruit, peeled, quartered and sliced
- Star fruit (also called carambola), sliced

Chicken Vegetable Soup

Choose and add vegetables and other ingredients to a pot of Rich Chicken Broth (page 11) or canned broth, to create your own special chicken vegetable soup.

- **Vegetables to cook in the broth:** chopped onions; sliced carrots, parsnips, celery or zucchini; shredded cabbage; diced turnips; frozen corn, peas or lima beans

- **Cooked or quick-cooking vegetables to add to the hot soup:** sautéed mushrooms, leeks or onions; chopped spinach or escarole; Chinese cabbage or snow pea pods; water chestnuts

Autumn and Winter Menu #6

Celery Rémoulade

CHICKEN BRAISED
WITH CIDER AND APPLES

Country Greens with Bacon
Red Potatoes in Their Jackets

Raisin Gingerbread Cake with Sour Cream Topping

This is a dinner I find particularly satisfying in its combination of colors, textures and tastes. The complete menu is perfect for an informal dinner party, while the chicken, greens and potatoes would make a very special family meal.

NOTES ON THE MENU

Since the Celery Rémoulade is served at table (as part of the meal), any hors d'oeuvre you decide to offer guests should be something very simple—perhaps crisp cheese sticks or Parmesan Toast (page 54). Onion Biscuits (page 61) or Drop Biscuits (page 21) would go very nicely with the main course.

• **Starches to cook in the broth or add, cooked, to the hot soup:** white or brown rice; small pasta; egg noodles; barley; diced potatoes

• **Herbs for flavoring:** chives, parsley, dill, tarragon, thyme, coriander

• **Garnishes to add before serving:** chopped scallions, tomatoes or hard-boiled egg; slices of lemon, avocado or cooked sausage; cubes of cooked chicken; croutons; matzo balls; wontons

For a thick soup, purée half the vegetables and stir into the broth; add a little cream, sour cream or plain yogurt, if you like.

CELERY REMOULADE

Makes enough for 6

This distinctive dish can be prepared one day ahead or, if you prefer, cook the celery root and make the sauce a day ahead and mix the two parts together six to eight hours before serving.

1 pound celery root
½ lemon
⅓ cup mayonnaise, or more to taste
Note: Homemade mayonnaise is usually recommended for this dish, but commercial mayonnaise may be used as well.
1½–2 teaspoons Dijon-style prepared mustard
1 tablespoon red wine vinegar

1½ teaspoons hot water
1½ teaspoons minced fresh tarragon or ½ teaspoon dried tarragon, powdered
1 tablespoon minced fresh chervil or flat-leaf (Italian) parsley
1½ tablespoons drained capers
1½ tablespoons minced cornichons (or gherkins)
Salt
Fresh pepper
Radicchio leaves

1. Trim both ends of the celery root and use a sharp knife to peel off the skin. Cut the celery root in matchsticks, discarding any woody parts (especially from the center). As you cut, drop the pieces into a bowl of water mixed with a squeeze of lemon juice; this will keep the celery root from discoloring.

Meanwhile, bring a pot of water to a boil.

2. Scoop the celery root into the boiling water and cover the pot to bring the water to a rolling boil again; uncover the pot and continue boiling for 1 min-

ute only. Drain the celery root and rinse immediately with cold water. Spread on paper towels to dry, then transfer to a large bowl.

3. Mix the remaining ingredients together to make a sauce, pour it over the matchsticks and mix gently. Add salt and pepper to taste and set aside in the refrigerator for at least 6 hours. The flavor takes a while to develop, so taste again before serving and adjust the seasoning if necessary.

Serve on leaves of radicchio.

CHICKEN BRAISED
WITH CIDER AND APPLES

Makes plenty for 6

Braising in wine, cider and cream produces succulent, flavorful chicken and apples. Always use a decent wine for cooking, something you'd be pleased to serve at table.

2 tablespoons butter
2 chickens, about 3 pounds each,
    cut into 8 serving pieces
1½ teaspoons salt
Fresh pepper
1 cup dry white wine

2 cups cider
5 tart-sweet cooking apples (such
    as Cortland, Rome Beauty,
    Gravenstein, Jonathan, etc.)
½ cup heavy cream

1. In a large skillet, melt the butter and sauté the chicken in 2 batches, until well browned. Return all the chicken pieces to the skillet and sprinkle with salt and pepper.

2. Pour the wine and cider over the chicken, cover tightly and simmer gently for 35 minutes.

Meanwhile, peel, quarter and core the apples; be careful to remove all the seeds and hard matter from the cores of the apples.

3. Add the apples to the skillet, spoon liquid over them and cover the skillet again. Simmer for another 15 minutes, or until the chicken and apples are tender. Arrange the chicken on an oven-proof serving platter, surrounded by the apples.

(At this point you may either cover and refrigerate the chicken until 30 minutes before serving or cover and keep it warm in a 300° oven while you make the sauce.)

4. Strain the liquid from the skillet into a small saucepan over medium heat and reduce the liquid by half. Skim off as much fat as possible and stir in the cream. Correct the seasoning if necessary.

If the chicken is hot and ready to serve, pour the hot sauce over it and serve immediately. If the chicken has been refrigerated, warm it (covered) for 30 minutes in a 325° oven, then gently heat the sauce, pour it over the chicken and serve.

COUNTRY GREENS WITH BACON

Makes about 5 cups

Chewy, tasty greens are spiked with the smoky flavor of good bacon and topped with crisp bacon bits. The dish starts with a marathon of leaf-rinsing that is best done early in the day so you'll have less to do at the cooking end.

2 pounds collard greens, kale or mustard greens, or a combination of 2 or 3 of these
Note: If you are cooking only kale, you will need 2½ pounds, since the thick center ribs will be removed.

½ pound thick-cut or slab bacon, cut in small dice
3 cloves garlic, minced
1½ tablespoons balsamic vinegar
Salt
Fresh pepper

1. Prepare the greens by discarding any yellowed leaves, trimming and discarding ½ inch of the stem ends of the mustard and collard greens and cutting out the thick center ribs of the kale. Wash the greens very well to remove dirt and sand; shake to remove excess water—what's left will be just enough water for steaming the greens.

Cut the remaining (still-attached) stems of the mustard and collard greens in ½-inch lengths and set them aside. Stack the mustard and collard leaves and cut into 1-inch pieces; tear the kale into bite-size pieces.

2. In a large kettle or casserole, cook the bacon until the fat is rendered and the bacon is crisp. Use a slotted spoon to remove the bacon bits; drain on paper towels. Set aside.

3. Put the garlic and stem pieces in the kettle and sauté for 2 minutes. Add the greens by the handful, stirring down as they wilt. When all the greens are wilted, add the vinegar and salt and pepper to taste and stir well. Cook, uncovered, over medium heat, stirring often, until the greens are chewy but tender, 5–10 more minutes.

(At this point, you may leave the greens in the refrigerator until just before you want to serve them. Reheat the greens over medium heat and proceed to step 4.)

4. Cover the kettle and let the greens steam for 5 more minutes over low heat. (You may have to add a bit more water to keep them from burning.) Transfer the greens to a warm bowl, sprinkle with bacon bits and serve hot.

RED POTATOES
IN THEIR JACKETS

Makes enough for 6

Potatoes, plain and simple, to go with the varied and interesting group of recipes in this menu.

24 small red potatoes
Note: If 4 potatoes per person is not enough for your crowd, prepare more and increase the butter and parsley proportionately.

3 tablespoons butter
3 tablespoons minced flat-leaf (Italian) parsley
Salt
Fresh pepper

1. Scrub the potatoes well and cut each in half. Boil in water to cover for 10–15 minutes, until tender.

2. Drain off the water, return the potatoes to the pot and shake briskly over medium heat to evaporate any remaining moisture. Add the butter, parsley and salt and pepper to taste. Mix well to melt the butter and coat the potatoes. Serve hot.

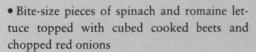

Cold-Weather Salads II

Here are some salad combinations to serve in autumn and winter, with cold or warm vinaigrette sauce:

• Bite-size pieces of spinach and romaine lettuce topped with cubed cooked beets and chopped red onions

• Mixed greens topped with beans (kidney, white, black, etc.), quartered cherry tomatoes, red pepper rings and shredded Jack cheese

• Sections of orange and grapefruit arranged on leaves of Bibb lettuce, with a generous sprinkling of raisins and chopped scallions.

• Shredded romaine lettuce and red cabbage tossed with slivers of sun-dried tomatoes and sliced mushrooms, sprinkled with Parmesan cheese

• Cubed apples and jícama on a bed of watercress, with crumbled blue cheese

• Chicory and romaine garnished with diced cooked potatoes, sliced radishes, cooked peas, chopped egg and bacon bits

RAISIN GINGERBREAD CAKE WITH SOUR CREAM TOPPING

Makes 1 round single layer cake

Buttermilk and raisins in the batter make a moist and delicious cake; sweetened sour cream topping turns it into something really special. Gingerbread can be an acquired taste, but I've noticed that this one seems to convert even the reluctant.

2 cups sifted cake flour
2 teaspoons baking powder
¼ teaspoon baking soda
2 teaspoons ground ginger
1 teaspoon cinnamon
½ teaspoon salt
⅓ cup (5⅓ tablespoons) butter, room temperature
½ cup sugar
1 egg

⅔ cup unsulfured molasses
¾ cup buttermilk
¾ cup dark raisins, tossed in a little flour

For the topping
1 cup sour cream
¼ teaspoon vanilla extract
2 tablespoons superfine sugar

1. Preheat the oven to 350°. Grease and flour a 9-inch round cake pan.

In a small bowl, whisk together the flour, baking powder, baking soda, spices and salt; set aside.

2. In a large bowl, cream the butter, then add the sugar and beat again until light. Add the egg and beat well. Add the molasses, blend well and beat for 1 minute at high speed.

3. Add the dry ingredients and buttermilk alternately, in 3 parts each, beating well after each addition. Beat for 1 more minute at high speed. Stir in the raisins. Pour the batter into the prepared pan.

4. Bake for 50–55 minutes, or until a cake tester inserted in the center of the cake comes out clean. Let the cake cool in the pan on a wire rack for 10 minutes, then turn out to finish cooling, right side up, on the rack.

Meanwhile, whisk together the topping ingredients until the sugar dissolves.

Serve the cake warm or cold, in wedges, with generous dollops of topping.

Autumn and Winter Menu #7

Wild Mushrooms on Toast

CHICKEN WITH CREAM SAUCE AND PARSLEY DUMPLINGS

Purée of Carrots and Parsnips
Lima Beans in Onion Sauce

Apple Crisp

In spite of the elegantly chic wild mushrooms, this is a down-home, old-fashioned supper—hearty, filling and delicious. It's not a menu I would attempt when speed was of the essence, but lots of it can and should be made ahead so you're not stuck forever in the kitchen—the supper isn't *that* old-fashioned!

NOTES ON THE MENU

If we're talking family meal here, I'm sure the kids can do without the mushrooms—wild mushrooms might be strictly for grown-up dinner parties. Aside from that, for family, you may simplify dessert by serving fresh apples and bakery cookies; for company, don't change a thing.

Easy Winter Appetizers

• Drained canned white beans mashed with garlic and a little olive oil, mixed with chopped red bell peppers and served with crackers, pita bread and raw vegetables

• Thin sheets of lavash (a Middle Eastern bread) spread with soft, herbed cheese, rolled up tightly and sliced into rounds

• Anchovy butter on toast triangles

• Good olives and crisp red radishes with black bread and sweet butter

WILD MUSHROOMS ON TOAST

Makes about 20 appetizers

Wild mushrooms have a wonderful, woodsy flavor, different from the cultivated white mushrooms we are accustomed to. They are expensive but worth a splurge, since only half a pound makes appetizers for six people.

½ pound fresh wild mushrooms
  (such as shiitake, cremini,
  chanterelle, oyster, etc.), woody
  stem ends trimmed
  *Note: If you like, use a
  combination of several kinds.*
4 tablespoons (½ stick) butter

20 slices high-quality white Italian
  or French bread, crusts removed
1 tablespoon minced shallots
Salt
Fresh pepper
Minced flat-leaf (Italian) parsley for
  garnish

1. Preheat the oven to 350°. Wipe the mushrooms clean (do not rinse them) and chop in small pieces.

Melt the butter in a skillet. Brush some of the melted butter on both sides of the bread and bake on a baking sheet for about 10 minutes, or until lightly crisped but not browned.

2. Add the shallots and mushrooms to the butter left in the skillet, season with salt and pepper and sauté over low heat for 5 minutes, or just until tender. Do not overcook.

3. Divide the mushrooms among the pieces of toast, top each piece with a pinch of minced parsley for garnish and serve hot.

More Easy Winter Appetizers

- Roasted peppers, sliced salami and provolone cheese cut in bite-size pieces to eat with Italian bread
- Smoked clams puréed with cream cheese, sour cream and horseradish, on crackers
- Taramasalata on slices of cold boiled potato, topped with chopped parsley
- Cubes of mozzarella wrapped in strips of prosciutto and skewered on toothpicks with seedless grapes

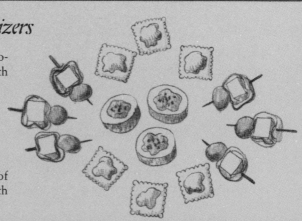

CHICKEN WITH CREAM SAUCE AND PARSLEY DUMPLINGS

Makes plenty for 6, with leftovers

Stick-to-the-ribs chicken with light, flavorful dumplings and a sauce that tastes creamy and rich but contains only a third of a cup of cream for more than six servings.

Note: There are a lot of steps in this recipe, so I encourage you to start a day ahead, preparing the chicken through step 1 and refrigerating it in the skillet overnight. Next day, heat the chicken and broth in the skillet and pick up where you left off.

3 tablespoons butter
¼ cup oil
2 chickens, about 3½ pounds each, each cut in 8 serving pieces and skinned
4¾ cups chicken broth
1 cup dry vermouth
1½ cups chopped onion (about 2 medium onions)
1 cup chopped carrot (about 2 medium carrots)
1 bay leaf
1 teaspoon salt

For the dumplings
¾ cup milk
1 egg
2 tablespoons minced flat-leaf (Italian) parsley
1 tablespoon butter or margarine, melted and cooled
2 cups flour
1 tablespoon baking powder
½ teaspoon salt

For the sauce
3 tablespoons flour
⅓ cup cream
Salt
Fresh pepper

1. Begin with the chicken: Melt 2 tablespoons of the butter with half the oil in a large skillet over medium heat. Sauté the chicken in batches, just until white or lightly browned all over, adding the remaining butter and oil as needed.

Return all the chicken to the skillet and add 3 cups of the broth, the vermouth, onions, carrots, bay leaf and salt. Cover and cook over low heat for 30–40 minutes, or until the chicken is tender. (After 20 minutes, move the lower layer of chicken pieces to the top.)

2. While the chicken is cooking, prepare the dumpling dough: In a large bowl, beat the milk and egg; whisk in the parsley and melted butter (or margarine). In a small bowl, stir together the flour, baking powder and salt. Gradually whisk the dry ingredients into the milk mixture, blending well. Set aside.

3. When the chicken is done, transfer the pieces to a large ovenproof platter; cover loosely with aluminum foil and keep warm in a 300° oven. Use a slotted spoon to remove and discard the vegetables and bay leaf from the broth.

Add 1 cup of the remaining broth and ½ cup water to the broth in the skillet. Bring the broth to a simmer.

4. Make the dumplings in two batches, working with half the dumpling dough at a time: Drop spoonfuls of dough (about the size of unshelled walnuts) from a wet tablespoon into the broth and simmer, uncovered, for 10 minutes.

Turn the dumplings over, cover the skillet and simmer for 10 more minutes. Remove the dumplings with a slotted spoon and arrange them on the platter around the chicken.

Add 1 cup water to the skillet, bring to a simmer and repeat the process with the remaining dough.

5. Make the sauce: With the heat low, sprinkle the remaining 3 tablespoons of flour on the broth remaining in the skillet. Stir briskly to blend, scraping up the brown bits on the bottom of the skillet. Cook for 2 minutes.

Gradually add ¾ cup of water, the remaining ¾ cup of chicken broth and the cream. Bring to a simmer, stirring constantly for a few minutes, and cook until slightly reduced and thickened. Season with salt and pepper to taste.

Pour half the sauce over the chicken and serve the remaining sauce on the side.

Christmas Spruce-Up

When you throw a Christmas party, get into the festive spirit by decking the halls, the living room and everywhere else with boughs of holly, garlands of greens and plenty of mistletoe.

• Hang a beautiful wreath on the front door to welcome your guests. Decorate the foyer with a small Christmas tree, and suspend a mistletoe kissing ball from the light fixture.

PUREE OF CARROTS AND PARSNIPS

Makes about 3½ cups

Naturally sweet and tasty, this could hardly be simpler to make, especially with the aid of a food processor for puréeing.

Note: You may make the purée ahead and reheat it just before serving.

1–1¼ **pounds carrots, trimmed and peeled**
1–1¼ **pounds parsnips, trimmed and peeled**
Note: Buy the fattest parsnips you can find; these have the greatest amount of sweet flesh surrounding the woody core.

2 **tablespoons butter**
⅓ **cup heavy cream**
Salt
Fresh pepper

1. Cut the carrots in ¼-inch slices. Cut off and discard the skinny ends of the parsnips; cut the parsnips in 2-inch chunks. Slice the tender flesh away from the woody core of each chunk of parsnip; discard the cores.

2. Simmer the carrots and parsnips in a covered saucepan half full of water for about 15 minutes, or until tender. Drain well.

3. Purée the carrots and parsnips with the butter and cream, adding salt and pepper to taste. Return the purée to the saucepan to reheat, stirring briskly over low heat. Serve hot.

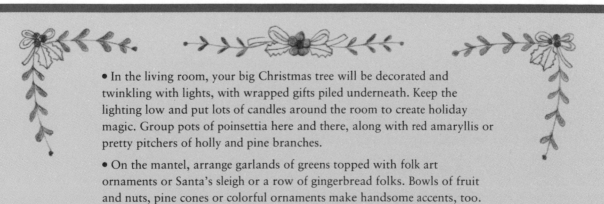

• In the living room, your big Christmas tree will be decorated and twinkling with lights, with wrapped gifts piled underneath. Keep the lighting low and put lots of candles around the room to create holiday magic. Group pots of poinsettia here and there, along with red amaryllis or pretty pitchers of holly and pine branches.

• On the mantel, arrange garlands of greens topped with folk art ornaments or Santa's sleigh or a row of gingerbread folks. Bowls of fruit and nuts, pine cones or colorful ornaments make handsome accents, too.

LIMA BEANS IN ONION SAUCE

Makes about 4½ cups

I usually prefer fresh vegetables to frozen, but fresh lima beans are always hard to find in my neighborhood. Fortunately, frozen baby limas are quite good and this dish makes excellent use of them.

Note: It may seem unusual to have both white wine and sherry in one recipe, but it works here.

4 tablespoons (½ stick) butter
1½ cups chopped onion (about
    2 medium onions)
⅓ cup white wine
⅓ cup chicken broth

4 cups frozen baby lima beans (two
    10-ounce packages)
Salt
3 tablespoons dry sherry
3 tablespoons white wine vinegar

1. In a large skillet over low heat, melt the butter and brown the onions slowly.

2. Add the wine, broth, lima beans and a sprinkling of salt and raise the heat while you break up and stir the frozen beans. Cover the pan, lower the heat and simmer until the limas are tender, about 15 minutes.

3. Uncover the skillet, add the sherry and vinegar and simmer for about 2 more minutes, until the sauce is reduced and thickened. Add more salt if needed.

Serve immediately or reheat in the skillet just before serving.

Hot Toddies

Make toddies in mugs or glasses warmed with very hot water.
Note: A jigger is 1½ ounces of liquid.

• **Hot Buttered Rum:** Combine 2 jiggers dark rum, a twist of lemon peel, a clove and a cinnamon stick. Add boiling cider and float a small pat of butter on top.

• **Hot Lemonade:** Stir together juice of ½ lemon, juice of ½ lime and 2 tablespoons superfine sugar. Add boiling water to taste, along with 1 jigger whiskey or rum, if desired.

• **Hot Milk Toddy:** Mix 1 jigger light rum, 1 jigger brandy and 1 teaspoon superfine sugar. Add hot milk and a sprinkling of nutmeg.

• **Hot Apple Toddy:** Mix 1 jigger applejack, 1 teaspoon superfine sugar, 2 cloves and a slice of lemon. Add boiling water to taste.

• **Hot Wine Cup:** Stir together ¼ cup red wine, juice of ½ lemon, 2 teaspoons superfine sugar and a twist of lemon peel. Add boiling water to taste.

APPLE CRISP

Makes plenty for 6, with leftovers

Dandy by itself, Apple Crisp is even better with heavy cream, softly whipped cream or vanilla or butter pecan ice cream. Leftovers are delicious for lunch the next day.

If you like, fix the Apple Crisp—baked or unbaked—the night before or in the morning and stash it in the refrigerator. Bring it to room temperature and pop it in the oven to warm or bake while you prepare or eat dinner.

2¼–2½ pounds cooking apples (such as McIntosh, Jonathan, Cortland, Rome Beauty, etc.)
1 cup sugar
¼ teaspoon ground cloves
¾ teaspoon cinnamon
1 tablespoon fresh lemon juice

1 cup plus 2 tablespoons flour
⅛ teaspoon salt
8 tablespoons (1 stick) butter
¾ cup chopped walnuts and/or pecans
Heavy cream, softly whipped cream or ice cream (optional)

1. Butter a shallow 1½- or 2-quart baking dish or casserole. Preheat the oven to 350° for a glass baking dish, 375° for a metal or ceramic dish.

Peel the apples and cut them in quarters. Cut out the cores, making sure to remove all the seeds and hard matter. Cut each quarter in 3 long slices and put the slices in a large bowl.

2. Add ¼ cup of the sugar, the cloves, cinnamon and lemon juice to the apples and mix well. Spread the apples in the baking dish.

3. Stir together the flour, salt and remaining ¾ cup of sugar. Cut the butter into the flour until the mixture has a crumbly texture. Stir in the nuts. Spread the mixture evenly on top of the apples.

4. Bake for 50–60 minutes, until the apples are tender and the crust is crisp and lightly browned. Serve warm, with heavy cream, whipped cream or ice cream, if you like.

Autumn and Winter Menu #8

SIMPLE SKILLET CHICKEN
WITH LEMON AND THYME

Corn Fritters
Baked Brussels Sprouts

Pecan Chocolate Squares
Sliced oranges

Good, solid food—not fancy or complicated—for family and friends: a dish of chicken braised with mixed dried fruit, plenty of fluffy fritters, cheese-sauced Brussels sprouts, and luscious cookies for dessert.

NOTES ON THE MENU

If you're in the mood for a little crunch, crisp greens would be a good starter for this menu. There are some jazzy salad suggestions on pages 24 and 77, but simple mixed lettuces (perhaps with Mustard Dressing, page 40) would be fine, too.

If company's coming (and even if they're not), you might want to follow the meal with a hot toddy (see page 132).

SIMPLE SKILLET CHICKEN
WITH LEMON AND THYME
Makes enough for 6

Light, easy to prepare and very attractive, with lemons around the edge of the platter and plump dried fruits tucked here and there among the chicken pieces. Only one skillet is used—no other pots and pans.

Note: I prefer to include both light and dark meat in this dish. If pieces are large, twelve will be enough; if small, make fifteen. If you prefer wings, you'll need eighteen, with wing tips removed.

¼ cup olive oil
12–18 pieces of chicken (any parts you like)
⅔ cup water
Juice of 1 lemon
1–1½ cups soft mixed dried fruit (pears, pitted prunes, apricots, apples, peaches)

¾ teaspoon powdered dried thyme
Salt
Fresh pepper
2 whole lemons, sliced thin, seeds removed

1. In a large skillet, heat the oil and lightly brown the chicken in batches. Set aside.

2. With the heat off, pour off most of the fat and add half of the water to the skillet. Stir well to loosen and dissolve the brown bits stuck to the skillet. Add the lemon juice, dried fruit, thyme and a sprinkling of salt and pepper and stir again. Arrange the chicken on the dried fruit and baste with the sauce. Arrange the lemon slices on the chicken.

3. Cover the skillet and cook over low heat for 30–40 minutes, basting occasionally, until the chicken is thoroughly cooked and the fruit is tender.

Remove the lemon slices and place them around the edge of a serving platter as a garnish. Transfer the chicken and fruit to the platter. Add the rest of the water to the skillet and heat, stirring, to make more sauce. Pour the sauce over the chicken and serve hot.

CORN FRITTERS

Makes about 35 small fritters

Fluffy little corn pancakes, crisp around the edges and soft inside, make a perfect accompaniment to Simple Skillet Chicken. These fritters are slightly sweet and very homey served plain or with honey or maple syrup.

Tip: For a different sort of fritter, omit the sugar from the recipe and add one savory ingredient instead—such as ½ cup of crumbled cooked bacon, a few tablespoons of chopped red or green pepper, two or three teaspoons of finely minced pickled jalapeño pepper or ¼ cup of minced scallions.

1 cup flour
1 teaspoon salt
2 teaspoons baking powder
1 tablespoon sugar
2 eggs
¾ cup milk

1¾ cups drained canned whole-kernel corn, puréed just until it resembles creamed corn (one 17-ounce can)
Note: Do not purée the corn too much; it should not be smooth.
Vegetable oil for frying (not olive oil)

1. In a small bowl, whisk together the flour, salt, baking powder and sugar. In a large bowl, beat the eggs and milk. Gradually add the dry ingredients, whisking as you add. Stir in the corn.

2. Heat ⅛ inch of oil in a heavy skillet. When the oil is very hot, drop tablespoons of batter into the skillet (don't crowd the pan) and fry on both sides until golden. Drain the fritters on paper towels and keep warm in a 300° oven. Repeat until all the batter is used, adding more oil as needed. Serve immediately.

BAKED BRUSSELS SPROUTS

Makes about 4½ cups

A hearty dish, made with creamy sauce, crumbs and cheese. It's not too Brussels-sprouty, so even those who are not keen on Brussels sprouts will love it. Make it ahead and reheat it, if you like.

1¼ **pounds fresh Brussels sprouts**
  (two 10-ounce containers)
¾ **cup milk**
¾ **cup chicken broth**
3 **tablespoons butter or margarine**
3 **tablespoons flour**

⅓ **cup grated Parmesan cheese**
  mixed with ⅓ **cup dry**
  breadcrumbs
Salt
Fresh pepper
⅛ **teaspoon ground nutmeg**

1. Have ready a 1½-quart baking dish or casserole, and preheat the oven to 375° for a glass baking dish, 400° for a metal or ceramic dish.

Cut off the stem ends of the sprouts and discard any yellow or wilted leaves. Cut the sprouts in quarters, rinse well and drain. Steam or parboil until barely crisp-tender, about 5 minutes. Drain and set aside.

Meanwhile, heat the milk and broth in a small saucepan.

2. In another small saucepan over low heat, melt the butter (or margarine), add the flour and cook, stirring constantly, for 1 minute. Add the hot milk and broth and stir until thick and smooth.

3. Combine the sprouts, sauce and half the cheese-crumb mixture in the baking dish and season well with salt, pepper and nutmeg. Sprinkle the remaining cheese-crumb mixture on top and bake for 20 minutes.

Serve hot from the oven or refrigerate the dish until serving time and then reheat in a 300° oven. (If you're doing the complete menu, reheat the sprouts while you're keeping the fritters warm.)

PECAN CHOCOLATE SQUARES

Makes 16 squares

The perfect indulgent finale for a simple menu, these layered confections (a sort of candy-cookie hybrid) are gooey and luscious and so rich that a small amount—like one—goes a long way. Store them in the refrigerator on warm days.

For the bottom layer
1¼ cups flour
¼ cup sugar
¼ cup (packed) light brown sugar
⅛ teaspoon salt
8 tablespoons (1 stick) cold butter, cut in pats

For the topping
2 eggs
½ cup light corn syrup
½ cup (packed) light brown sugar

2 tablespoons butter, melted and cooled
1 teaspoon vanilla extract
¼ teaspoon salt
¾ cup chopped toasted pecans (see page 23 for toasting instructions)
½ cup chocolate chips or mini chocolate chips

1. Preheat the oven to 350°; grease and flour a 9-inch-square baking pan.

Make the bottom layer: In a bowl or a food processor, mix the flour, sugar, brown sugar and salt. Add the butter and cut it in until the mixture has the texture of breadcrumbs. Pat the mixture evenly into the prepared pan. Bake for 15 minutes and place the pan on a wire rack to cool.

2. Make the topping: In a medium bowl, whisk together all the topping ingredients except the pecans and chocolate. Stir in the pecans and chocolate.

3. Pour the topping over the cooled dough in the pan, and use a spatula or spoon to spread the nuts and chocolate evenly.

4. Bake for 45 minutes, or until the top looks crisp and set and slightly puffed. Allow to cool in the pan on a wire rack, then run a knife around the edges to loosen them. Cut in squares as you would brownies.

Autumn and Winter Menu #9

Cool Carrot-Peanut Soup

CHICKEN CURRY
WITH CONDIMENTS

Cucumber Raita
Spiced Banana Raita
Basmati rice

Fruit sherbet

The pleasure of a curry meal is in sampling the condiments and raitas in combination with the chicken and rice. Pile your plate with plenty of rice, add chicken and sauce, arrange spoonfuls of each condiment and raita on the side—and taste your way around the plate.

Tip: Beer is the drink of choice for curry.

Note: Basmati is an Indian variety of long-grain white rice, with a nutty, toasty taste. It is particularly appropriate for this meal, but of course you may serve your usual long-grain white rice if you prefer. Cook Basmati rice the same way you'd cook any long-grain white rice.

NOTES ON THE MENU

Be sure you read More Condiments for Chicken Curry on page 140 before you decide just which ones you want to try.

COOL CARROT-PEANUT SOUP

Makes 6 servings

One of the world's easiest-to-make soups, using the simplest ingredients. Though this is not an Indian soup—it has Caribbean origins—it complements an Indian-style curry meal.

Tip: Each serving is small, meant only to whet your appetite, not to fill you up before the generous and varied dishes that follow in this menu.

1½ pounds carrots, peeled, trimmed and chunked
4½ cups vegetable or chicken broth mixed with ½ cup water
10 tablespoons (½ cup plus 2 tablespoons) smooth or crunchy peanut butter

1 teaspoon superfine sugar (optional)
Minced parsley and chopped roasted unsalted peanuts for garnish

1. Simmer the carrots, uncovered, in the diluted broth for 30 minutes. Purée the cooked carrots with the broth and peanut butter (in batches if necessary) until completely smooth. Be sure all the peanut butter is blended in.

2. Refrigerate the soup until cool but not icy. Taste and then add the sugar only if needed—for example, if the carrots were not very sweet and the peanut butter contained no sugar.

Sprinkle with parsley and chopped peanuts and serve.

More Condiments for Chicken Curry

• Onion Chutney (makes about 1½ cups): Peel and chop 1 medium red onion and 1 medium yellow onion; mix in a bowl with ½ teaspoon chopped ginger, ¼ teaspoon salt, 1 teaspoon sugar, ⅓ cup rice vinegar, and a pinch (or more) of hot pepper flakes. Let stand for 1 hour before serving. Add salt to taste.

• Sliced oranges sprinkled with wine vinegar and cinnamon

• Chopped toasted almonds

• Spicy Lentils (makes 2½ cups): Slice and sauté 1 large yellow onion in 2 tablespoons butter; add ¼ teaspoon turmeric, ¼ teaspoon chili powder, 2 cups *cooked* lentils and 1¼ cups water. Cook, stirring and mashing slightly, until thick, about 15 minutes. Add salt to taste.

• Ripe avocados, sliced and brushed with lemon or lime juice

• Dried currants, soaked in port wine

CHICKEN CURRY
WITH CONDIMENTS

Makes plenty for 6

For maximum enjoyment of curry, have at least several condiments to go with it. (Sweet Tomato Chutney [page 31] is delicious with this curry.) The recipe makes a lot of sauce, which is meant to go on the accompanying rice—almost a meal in itself.

Juice of 2 small lemons plus grated
    rind of 1 of the lemons
    Note: Grate the rind first; keep
    the rind and juice separate
3 whole boneless chicken breasts,
    skinned and cut in 1-inch pieces
¼ cup flour stirred with
    ½ teaspoon salt, for coating the
    chicken
4 tablespoons (½ stick) butter
3 tablespoons vegetable oil (not
    olive oil)
1½ cups chopped onion (about
    2 medium onions)
1 large tart cooking apple, peeled,
    cored and chopped
    Note: Use an apple that is not
    too firm, such as Cortland,
    Rome Beauty, etc., rather than
    Granny Smith or Winesap

3 plum tomatoes, cored and
    chopped (about ½ pound)
1 tablespoon minced garlic
2 tablespoons flour
3 tablespoons mild or medium-hot
    curry powder
    Note: If you prefer, make
    your own fresh curry powder
    by combining 2 teaspoons
    each turmeric and paprika,
    1 teaspoon each ground
    ginger, cayenne, cumin and
    coriander, ½ teaspoon each
    cinnamon and black pepper and
    ¼ teaspoon ground cloves.
2½ cups chicken broth
½ cup cream or half-and-half
Salt
Condiments (instructions follow)

1. Pour half the lemon juice over the chicken and mix well. Spread the chicken on wax paper, sprinkle with the salted flour and toss the chicken to coat it with flour.

2. Heat the butter and oil in a large skillet over medium heat, add the chicken and sauté for 20 minutes. Stir often, scraping the browned flour from the skillet. With a slotted spoon, transfer the chicken to a 2-quart casserole and set aside.

3. Add the onions to the butter and oil in the skillet and sauté over low heat until soft. Add the apple and tomatoes and continue cooking until the apple is soft enough to mash. Turn off the heat, add the garlic, the 2 tablespoons of unsalted flour and the curry powder and use the back of a wooden spoon to mash everything to a rough paste.

With the heat still off, gradually add the chicken broth and cream, stirring well to blend and to get the brown bits off the pan.

4. Preheat the oven to 350°. Bring the sauce to a boil, reduce the heat and simmer, stirring constantly, for 10 minutes. Add the remaining lemon juice, the grated lemon rind and salt to taste. Stir the sauce into the chicken in the casserole, cover tightly and bake for 45 minutes.

Serve hot, with plenty of rice and a selection of condiments.

CONDIMENTS

Six condiments (either all of the ones described below or some of these plus some from page 140) make chicken curry into a lavish meal. If you're short on time, opt for three basics—chutney, scallions and chopped nuts—and double the amounts given; if you're feeling expansive, you may certainly prepare more than six. Put each condiment in a separate bowl, with a spoon; eat them with the curry and rice.

- 1 jar mango or other fruit chutney
  Note: Sweet Tomato Chutney (page 31) is a delicious one you can make yourself, if you have time.

- 3 scallions, white and green parts, trimmed and sliced thin

- ¾ cup unsalted roasted peanuts, chopped

- ¾ cup unsweetened flaked or shredded coconut, toasted
  Note: To toast, spread coconut on an ungreased baking sheet in a preheated 350° oven for 5–10 minutes, stirring occasionally, until lightly browned and crisp.

- ¾ cup golden raisins soaked in ½ cup brandy

- 8 strips bacon, cooked crisp, drained and crumbled

CUCUMBER RAITA

Makes 2½–3 cups

The mild heat, intense flavor and rough texture of curry are best appreciated when set off by contrasting (and soothing) yogurt-based raitas.

2 medium cucumbers, trimmed, peeled and seeded
1 cup plain (unflavored) yogurt
2 tablespoons minced fresh coriander
Salt
Fresh pepper

Dice the cucumbers and stir them with the yogurt and coriander. Add salt to taste and a good grinding of pepper. Chill and serve, garnished with a few coriander leaves.

SPICED BANANA RAITA

Makes about 1¾ cups

1 tablespoon butter
⅛ teaspoon each ground nutmeg, cloves, cinnamon and cumin

Fresh pepper
2 large ripe bananas
¾ cup plain (unflavored) yogurt

1. In a small skillet over low heat, melt the butter, add the spices and a grinding of fresh pepper and stir for 1 minute. Add 1 banana, mashing it into the butter and spices.

2. Turn off the heat and allow the mixture to cool while you dice the second banana. Combine the mashed banana mixture, yogurt and diced banana and stir well. Chill and serve.

Autumn and Winter Menu #10

Chile con Queso with Corn Tortilla Chips and Crudités

CHICKEN WITH SOUR CREAM AND CORIANDER SAUCE

Drunken Beans
Baked Bananas
Salsa Cruda
Hot Flour Tortillas

Mocha Custard
Fruit bowl

A festive meal and one of my all-time favorites. You can, in fact, easily turn this dinner into a party by doubling or tripling the recipes and inviting twelve or eighteen hungry friends in to sample the results.

Tip: This makes a good cooperative dinner, too, if you divide the recipes among volunteer chefs and bring the ready-to-eat dishes to the most centrally located home.

NOTES ON THE MENU

For a simpler family meal, skip the Chile con Queso (but please do try it another time as an hors d'oeuvre) and serve a green salad, followed by the chicken with beans, tortillas and salsa. Serve bakery cookies or fruit for dessert.

CHILE CON QUESO
WITH CORN TORTILLA CHIPS
AND CRUDITES

Makes about 5 cups

Chile con Queso is a hot dip in both senses—spicy because of the jalapeños and, also, brought to your family or guests straight from the stove. The recipe makes a lot of dip, but leftovers are delicious on macaroni, spread on sandwiches or mixed into scrambled eggs.

Note: It may surprise you to see an ingredient like Velveeta processed cheese food here, but it does make a very good Chile con Queso.

1½ cups canned whole tomatoes with juice (one 14-ounce can)

2 tablespoons corn or other vegetable oil (not olive oil)

4 tablespoons (½ stick) butter

1½ cups chopped onion (about 2 medium or 1 large onion)

1 cup canned chopped mild green chilies (two 4-ounce cans)

2 pickled jalapeños, stemmed and minced

Note: If you like really hot and spicy food, use 3 or even 4 jalapeños.

1 5-ounce can evaporated milk

1 pound Velveeta processed cheese food, cut in ½-inch cubes

½ pound Jack cheese or Longhorn cheddar cheese, shredded

1 small jícama, peeled, sliced ¼ inch thick and then cut in ½-inch-wide strips

2 heads Belgian endive, trimmed and separated into leaves

1 medium zucchini, trimmed and cut in small fingers

1 red bell pepper, stemmed, seeded, deveined and cut in ½-inch strips

1 8- or 10-ounce bag of unsalted corn tortilla chips

1. Drain the tomatoes and reserve the juice; chop the tomatoes in ¼-inch pieces.

In a large skillet or heavy saucepan, heat the oil and butter and sauté the onions over low heat, until very soft. Add the tomatoes, ¼ cup of the reserved tomato juice, the green chilies, jalapeños and evaporated milk. Cook over low heat, stirring often, for 5 minutes.

2. Still over low heat, add the cheeses by the handful, stirring until each handful melts.

3. Turn off the heat and cover the Chile con Queso to keep it hot while you arrange the raw vegetables attractively on a plate.

Transfer the Chile con Queso to a chafing dish or casserole over a candle warmer or on a warming tray. (If you don't have either, put the hot dip in the top pan of a double boiler, with boiled water in the bottom pan.) Serve with the plate of crudités and a bowl of corn tortilla chips.

CHICKEN WITH SOUR CREAM AND CORIANDER SAUCE

Makes enough for 6

This nicely browned chicken with herb-flecked sauce earns enthusiastic reviews from friends. If necessary, keep it warm in the oven while you put the finishing touches on the rest of the meal.

Vegetable oil for browning
2 chickens, about 3½ pounds each,
    each cut in 8 serving pieces, or
    16 assorted chicken parts
Salt
Fresh pepper
2 cups chicken broth

1 cup (packed) flat-leaf (Italian)
    parsley leaves
3 cloves garlic, halved
1 small onion, quartered
1 cup sour cream
½ cup (packed) fresh coriander
    leaves, minced

1. Heat a little oil in a large skillet. Brown the chicken pieces in batches, sprinkling with salt and pepper. (This will take some time.) The chicken should be thoroughly cooked.

2. In a food processor, purée all the remaining ingredients except the coriander to make a sauce. Set aside.

3. Pour off the fat from the skillet (but keep the browned bits). Put all the chicken in the skillet and pour the sour cream sauce over it, making sure the pieces are well moistened. Cover and very slowly bring to a simmer. Uncover the skillet and cook gently for 15 minutes, spooning sauce over the chicken several times.

4. Remove the chicken (but not the sauce) to an ovenproof platter, cover lightly with foil and keep warm in a 300° oven for up to 30 minutes. Continue simmering the sauce for 10 minutes, stirring often, to reduce it. Just before serving add the minced coriander and stir well. Pour the hot sauce over the chicken and serve immediately.

DRUNKEN BEANS

Makes about 4 cups

Beer in this recipe gives the beans a subtle yet robust flavor. Make the beans ahead, if that's more convenient.

1½ cups chopped onion (about
   2 medium onions)
Vegetable oil (not olive oil)
6 cups canned pinto beans (three
   1-pound cans)

1½ cups beer (one 12-ounce bottle)
¼ teaspoon hot red pepper flakes
¾ teaspoon salt
1 teaspoon sugar

1. In a large skillet or saucepan, brown the onion in a little oil. While the onions are browning, turn all the beans into a strainer or colander and rinse well with cold running water. Shake out the excess water.

2. Put 1 cup of the beans into the skillet or saucepan and mash well with a fork or potato masher. Add the remaining beans and the rest of the ingredients. Blend well and simmer, covered, for 30 minutes, stirring occasionally. Un-cover and simmer over very low heat for 20 more minutes, stirring often. You may have to add a bit of water to keep the beans from burning. When the beans are done, add salt to taste and just enough water to achieve the consistency you like best.

Serve hot or refrigerate for later use. At serving time either warm the beans over low heat (stirring often, and adding a little water, if needed, to keep the beans from burning) or in a 325° oven for 20 minutes.

Quick and Easy Desserts

When there's no time to prepare homemade dessert, put together an almost-instant treat from the choices below.

- Spread blueberry jam on slices of bakery sponge cake; top with defrosted frozen blueberries and sweetened whipped cream.
- Serve pecans and pistachios, almonds, fancy glacé fruits, with liqueur or sweet wine.
- Serve small scoops of fruit sherbet over sliced oranges and pineapple.
- Sprinkle cinnamon sugar on toasted slices of storebought pound cake, and melt under broiler; serve with vanilla or coffee ice cream.
- Slice bananas lengthwise and sauté in butter, brown sugar and a little rum.

BAKED BANANAS

Makes enough for 6

A bit different from the usual fried banana slices and they take just a short time to make. You may prepare the baked bananas ahead and reheat them before serving.

6 slightly underripe bananas (with green tips)
2 tablespoons butter or margarine, melted

¼ teaspoon cinnamon mixed with 1 tablespoon sugar

1. Preheat the oven to 350°. Peel the bananas and cut them on the diagonal on ½-inch-thick slices. Brush a jellyroll or sheetcake pan with some of the melted butter or margarine and arrange the banana slices in a single layer on the pan.

2. Brush the tops of the slices with the remaining butter or margarine, sprinkle evenly with the cinnamon-sugar mix and bake for 20 minutes. Serve immediately or, if you prepare the bananas ahead of time, reheat them in a 325° oven for 10 minutes.

Mix–and–Match Menus

Three Stuffed Vegetables (page 100)

Chicken Braised with Cider and Apples (page 123)
Corn Fritters (page 136)
Lima Beans in Onion Sauce (page 132)

Pecan Chocolate Squares (page 138)

Tangy Greens with Fresh Croutons (page 153)
Simple Skillet Chicken with Lemon and Thyme (page 135)
Savory Lentils (page 156)

Walnut-Honey Cake (page 163)

SALSA CRUDA

Makes about 2¾ cups

When I make salsa in summer, I use ripe, juicy tomatoes. In winter, canned tomatoes—which are used in this recipe—are far preferable to those round red things alleged to be fresh tomatoes. Make the salsa one day ahead so the flavor has time to develop; leftovers keep for up to three weeks in the refrigerator.

8 cups canned Italian-style whole tomatoes (two 35-ounce cans)
½ cup canned chopped mild green chilies (one 4-ounce can)
2 roasted fresh jalapeños, peeled, seeded and sliced (see page 54), or 2 pickled jalapeños, stemmed and sliced
2 cloves garlic, quartered

1 medium red onion, chunked, or 4 scallions, white and green parts, trimmed and cut in 1-inch pieces
2 tablespoons red wine vinegar or 2 tablespoons liquid from pickled jalapeños
Note: Use the pickled jalapeño liquid if you like especially hot, spicy salsa.
2 tablespoons olive oil
Salt

1. Drain the tomatoes in a colander or strainer, then halve them, rinse away the seeds and drain again. Chop the drained tomatoes by hand, in ½-inch pieces. Set aside.

2. Put the remaining ingredients except the salt in the bowl of a food processor and process in pulses, just until all the ingredients are minced. Transfer to a large bowl, add the chopped tomatoes and mix well; season with salt to taste.

Spoon the salsa into jars, cover the jars and store in the refrigerator.

HOT FLOUR TORTILLAS

Makes plenty for 6

12 or more 8- or 10-inch flour tortillas, fresh or frozen

Note: Storebought tortillas are convenient and perfectly acceptable.

To prepare fresh tortillas, simply divide them in 2 stacks, wrap each stack tightly in foil and leave in a 325° oven until very hot, about 20 minutes. To prepare frozen tortillas, spread them out (not touching each other) to defrost, then proceed as with fresh ones.

Remove the foil from one stack at a time and serve the hot tortillas wrapped snugly in a cotton or linen napkin, on a plate or in a basket.

MOCHA CUSTARD

Makes plenty for 6

A delicately flavored custard, with a thin chocolate layer on the bottom (it's on the top while the custard bakes) and an irresistibly silky texture.

2 cups whole milk
2 squares (2 ounces) semisweet chocolate, chopped
1 tablespoon instant coffee granules

3 eggs
1¾ cups sweetened condensed milk (one 14-ounce can)
1 tablespoon vanilla extract

1. Preheat the oven to 325°; butter a 1-quart casserole or baking dish and bring a kettle of water to a boil.

Heat the whole milk just to the point where bubbles begin to form around the sides of the pan. Add the chopped chocolate and coffee granules and stir until melted and blended into the milk. Little bits of chocolate will remain (these will form a thin layer of chocolate on the baked custard). Set aside to cool, stirring occasionally to release heat and keep the mixture smooth.

2. Beat the eggs and pour them through a strainer into a large bowl. Add the sweetened condensed milk, vanilla and cooled chocolate mixture and stir very gently, until well blended. Gentle stirring helps to avoid incorporating air into the mixture, which in turn yields a smooth-textured custard.

Pour the mixture into the prepared casserole.

3. Place the casserole in a larger pan (for instance, a roasting pan) on the middle rack of the oven. Carefully pour 1 inch of boiling water into the larger pan to make a hot water bath for the casserole.

Bake for 75–85 minutes, or until a knife inserted in the custard comes out almost clean. Carefully lift the casserole out of the larger pan and place it on a wire rack; let the custard cool to room temperature.

4. Run a sharp knife around the edge, cover tightly with an inverted serving platter and turn over quickly to unmold. (The top of the custard may crack when you unmold it. If this worries you, wait until the custard has cooled, then conceal the crack by spreading or piping the top with slightly sweetened whipped cream garnished with a dusting of cinnamon.)

Refrigerate the custard until it's needed; serve cool or at room temperature.

Step-by-Step Holiday Party Planner

1. Make guest list; send or telephone invitations. Keep track of RSVPs.

2. Plan menu and drinks. Make shopping lists for food, beverages, nonfood items (paper goods, candles, ice, etc.).

3. One week before: Order special items (flowers, liquor, etc.); order rental tables, coat racks. Plan table or buffet arrangement to be sure you have enough platters, china, glasses, silver, vases, etc.; if not, borrow or rent. Check tablecloths, placemats, napkins; borrow or rent more if needed. Buy nonperishable foods and nonfood items.

4. Three days before: Clean house. Remove family coats from coat closet; supply enough hangers for guests. Put towels and soap in guest bathroom.

5. Two days before: Shop for perishables. Prepare dishes or ingredients that can be stored. Set buffet or dining table; decorate house (candles, greens, etc.). Set up bar.

6. Day before: Prepare more food.

7. Day of party: Everyone does assigned chores (pick up rented equipment, flowers, ice; give house final straightening, etc.). Prepare food. Take bath; calm down; enjoy party!

Autumn and Winter Menu #11

Tangy Greens with Fresh Croutons

CHICKEN BREASTS STUFFED WITH SAUSAGE AND PINE NUTS

Savory Lentils
Sweet and Sour Beets

Hazelnut Tart with Whipped Cream

This bistro-style meal of simple, unpretentious foods with good, strong flavors translates into a sophisticated dinner. And, happily, it's one that can be almost entirely prepared ahead, if you read the recipes carefully and do a bit of advance planning.

NOTES ON THE MENU

It's pleasant to begin a dinner party with an hors d'oeuvre—find one in the suggestions on pages 127 and 128. My husband likes a round French country loaf with this meal, and he always appreciates a bowl of fruit as an alternative to the rich dessert.

Fruit and Cheese Combinations

Be sure to bring the cheese to room temperature before serving.

- Sweet or tart apples with smoked Gouda, Gruyère or sharp New York or Vermont cheddar
- Plums with provolone or Lancashire
- Red, green or black grapes with Stilton, Jarlsberg or Emmentaler
- Fresh figs with Mascarpone or Cheshire
- Dried figs with high-quality feta
- Oranges or tangerines with Bel Paese or Saga blue
- Pears with Bleu de Bresse, Brie or Camembert
- Mangos with Petit Suisse or L'Explorateur

TANGY GREENS
with FRESH CROUTONS

Makes enough for 6

Watercress and arugula give a peppery kick to this salad. And if you've never tasted them before, you'll find that homemade croutons are much better than packaged ones.

12 slices good-quality French or
Italian bread, ½-inch thick and
2½ inches in diameter, crusts
removed
Olive oil
Salt
Fresh pepper
Powdered dried basil or oregano

Freshly grated Parmesan cheese
3 cups (packed) watercress sprigs
and leaves
3 cups (packed) bite-size pieces
arugula
3 cups (packed) bite-size pieces red
leaf, Bibb or Boston lettuce
Garlic Vinaigrette Sauce (page 95)

1. Make the croutons: Preheat the oven to 350°. Arrange the bread in 1 layer on a cutting board and brush olive oil lightly on the tops and sides. Sprinkle with pinches of salt, pepper and powdered oregano or basil. Turn the slices over and repeat, adding a sprinkling of grated cheese. Pat the cheese onto the slices so it sticks.

Cut each slice in 8 pieces, place the pieces cheese side up on a baking sheet and bake for 10–15 minutes, or until dry and lightly crisp. Do not overbake.

cut in eight pieces

2. Just before serving, put the greens in a large salad bowl, dress with Garlic Vinaigrette Sauce and toss well. Sprinkle croutons on the salad and toss again.

CHICKEN BREASTS STUFFED WITH *SAUSAGE* AND *PINE NUTS*

Makes enough for 6

The recipe makes ten stuffed breasts, each one plump and very filling—which should be plenty to feed six people with appetites ranging from small to large. (On the other hand, one of my dinner guests, a wonderful—and slim—cook himself, ate four stuffed breasts at a sitting.)

5 whole boneless chicken breasts,
   skinned and halved
Salt
Fresh pepper
¾–1 pound sweet Italian pork
   sausage
Vegetable oil
3 cloves garlic, minced
2 teaspoons paprika

¼ cup (packed) minced flat-leaf
   (Italian) parsley
¼ cup toasted pine nuts (see page
   23 for toasting instructions)
1½ cups white wine
Flour
2 tablespoons butter
2 tablespoons olive oil

1. Pull off the long, narrow pointed piece of chicken that is loosely attached to the underside of each half breast. These pieces are not needed here, so refrigerate or freeze them for another use.

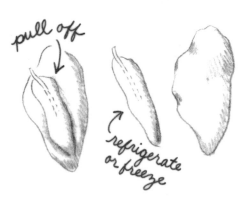

Pound each half breast to about ⅛–³⁄₁₆ inch thick. Try not to tear or break through the flesh, but if you do, it is easy to fill any holes since the flesh is pliable and sticky. Sprinkle with salt and pepper and set aside.

2. Make the stuffing: Discard the sausage casings. Heat a little vegetable oil in a skillet, add the sausage meat, garlic and paprika and sauté, stirring to break up the sausage, until the pork is well cooked. Drain on paper towels.

Chop the cooked sausage mixture in pea-sized bits and transfer to a bowl. Mix with the parsley, pine nuts and 2 tablespoons of the wine.

3. On a piece of wax paper, divide the stuffing in 10 portions. Place a portion in the center of a chicken cutlet. Fold the end of the cutlet over the stuffing, fold the sides in and roll it over, ending seam side down. Repeat for all cutlets.

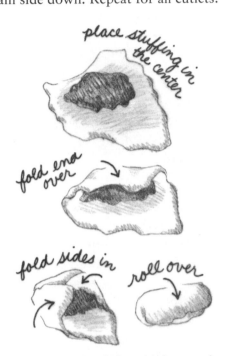

place stuffing in the center

fold end over

fold sides in

roll over

Don't worry if the chicken cutlets are a bit torn and some stuffing is popping out; the flour coating and the sautéing will hold each little package together.

4. Pat flour all over each stuffed breast; dust off excess flour. In a large skillet, melt the butter and olive oil over low heat. Arrange the stuffed breasts in a single layer and sauté until lightly browned; turn and brown on the other side.

5. Set aside ½ cup of the wine and add what remains to the skillet. Cover and simmer the chicken over low heat for 10 minutes, until tender and thoroughly heated. Transfer the chicken to an oven-proof serving platter, cover it lightly with foil and either keep it warm in a low oven while you make the sauce or refrigerate until needed.

6. Add the set-aside ½ cup of wine to the skillet and simmer until reduced to about ¾ cup. Strain the sauce and season to taste with salt and pepper.

Note: By itself, the sauce is quite strong in flavor; over the chicken, you'll find it is just right.

If the chicken is keeping warm in the oven, pour the sauce over it and serve immediately. If you have made the chicken ahead, refrigerate the sauce, too, until dinner. Then reheat the chicken in a 325° oven (with the foil cover on) and warm the sauce in a saucepan. Pour the hot sauce over the hot chicken and serve.

SAVORY LENTILS

Makes about 4½ cups

If possible, make this lentil salad the day before you want to serve it, to give the flavors time to blend.

1½ cups dried lentils (about
    10 ounces)
    *Note: Use the widely available
    brownish-green lentils, not the
    less common red ones.*
1¾ cups chicken broth
4½ cups water
6 tablespoons fruity olive oil

Juice of 1 medium lime (about
    2 tablespoons)
2 tablespoons Dijon-style prepared
    mustard
Salt
Fresh pepper
5 scallions, white and green parts,
    trimmed and sliced as thin as
    possible

1. Pick over the lentils and discard any pebbles and shriveled lentils. Rinse well in a strainer. Put the lentils, chicken broth and water in a saucepan, cover the pan and bring to a boil. Stir, cover again and lower the heat. Simmer 20–25 minutes, or until firm but thoroughly cooked. Transfer to a strainer to drain.

2. In a medium bowl, whisk the olive oil, lime juice, mustard and a little salt and pepper. Stir in the scallions. Add the warm lentils and stir well. Taste and correct the seasoning with more salt and pepper. Store in the refrigerator overnight, if possible, or for several hours, stirring occasionally.

Bring the lentils to room temperature before serving.

The Christmas Table

The Christmas dinner table should be especially festive, with pretty tablecloth and napkins, polished glassware and flatware, your favorite serving platters. Here are some tabletop decorating ideas to choose from.

- In the center of the tablecloth: white lace runner; red and green plaid napkins with corners overlapped; mirrored tray; pine wreath, lying flat; garland of greens

- At each place setting: a little basket of chocolates or glacé fruits; a small gift; a gingerbread man or woman; a pretty tree ornament

SWEET AND SOUR BEETS

Makes about 4½ cups

I know fresh beets are a pain in the neck to prepare—they have to be peeled, they're hard to cut and they stain your fingers purple. But it's worth the trouble because the flavor of fresh beets is incomparable.

Note: This dish can be made a day ahead and then reheated, covered, in a 325° oven for 15 minutes or even faster on top of the stove in a saucepan with a little water added to keep the beets from burning.

1 cup water
⅔ cup red wine vinegar
2½ tablespoons sugar
½ teaspoon salt

10 medium beets, trimmed, peeled
   and cut in ½-inch cubes
   (2¼–2½ pounds without stems
   and leaves)

1. Put the first four ingredients in a heavy nonreactive saucepan (stainless steel, enameled, etc.), cover and bring to a boil, stirring to dissolve the sugar.

2. Add the beets and stir well. Lower the heat, tilt the lid slightly so steam can escape and simmer, stirring occasionally, for 30–35 minutes until the beets are barely tender.

3. Remove the lid and continue simmering over low heat, stirring occasionally, until almost all the liquid is gone and the beets are lightly glazed, about 15–20 minutes.

Serve hot in winter, cold in summer.

- Instead of using napkin rings, tie napkins with: green velvet bows (and tie bows around candlesticks, too); gold and silver cord; red plaid taffeta ribbons with a sprig of holly or pine tucked into each bow
- For the centerpiece: arrangement of greens, pinecones and red berries; lots of small, wrapped gifts piled in a basket or on a tray; bowls of shiny Christmas tree ornaments; lots of chubby red and white candles

HAZELNUT TART
WITH WHIPPED CREAM

Makes 1 round tart

A delectable tart with a crisp, sugary top and crunchy hazelnut filling on a rich crust. Make it in a 10½-inch round tart pan with a removable bottom.

Note: Be sure your hazelnuts are fresh; stale nuts will ruin the flavor of the tart.

For the tart shell
1½ cups flour
3 tablespoons sugar
8 tablespoons (1 stick) cold butter
1 egg yolk stirred with 1 table-
    spoon cream

For the filling
1½ cups whole hazelnuts, toasted
    and skinned (see page 23 for
    toasting and skinning
    instructions)

8 tablespoons (1 stick) butter,
    melted and cooled
½ cup superfine sugar
3 egg yolks
Pinch of salt
6 tablespoons heavy cream

½ cup heavy cream stirred with
    1 tablespoon confectioner's or
    superfine sugar

1. Make the tart dough: Stir together the flour and sugar. Cut in the butter with a pastry blender or food processor, until the mixture looks like coarse meal. Add the egg yolk mixture and blend just until the dough forms a ball. Flatten the ball of dough into a disk, wrap well and refrigerate for 1 hour.

2. Preheat the oven to 425°.

Make the tart shell: Roll out the dough between pieces of plastic wrap, to a 12½-inch circle. (If the dough is too cold to roll out, wait just until it is pliable.) Peel the top piece of plastic away and invert the dough onto the tart pan.

Press the dough firmly into the pan and then peel off the remaining piece of plastic. Patch the dough, filling in any bare spots, and trim the edges. Prick the dough all over with a fork, at ¼-inch intervals.

3. Partially bake the tart shell: Line the tart shell with foil, covering it completely, including the top edges, and bake for 5 minutes. Reduce the heat to 400°, remove the foil and continue baking for 10 more minutes. Let the shell cool in the pan on a wire rack. Reduce the heat to 350° in preparation for baking the filled tart shell.

4. Make the filling: Coarsely chop half of the hazelnuts; grind the remaining half to a medium-coarse texture (a food processor works well for this). Beat together the butter, sugar, egg yolks and salt. Stir in the nuts. Whip the 6 tablespoons of cream and fold it gently into the butter mixture. Spread the filling evenly in the partially baked tart shell.

5. Place the tart on a baking sheet on the lowest shelf of the oven and bake for 25 minutes, or until the top of the filling is golden brown and crisp and the tart shell is a light tan. Let the tart cool completely in the pan on a wire rack.

Carefully lift out the tart on the removable bottom (it cracks easily) and place it, with the metal bottom, on a flat serving platter or tray.

Whip the sweetened heavy cream to soft peaks and serve with the tart.

Autumn and Winter Menu #12

Eggplant Dip with Toasted Pita Bread

MIDDLE EASTERN
YOGURT-BAKED CHICKEN LEGS

Cucumber, Chick Pea and Red Onion Salad
White or brown rice

Walnut-Honey Cake
Grapes

This is a very healthy meal, as I understand the concept, but it's unlikely that anyone will even notice because it tastes so good.

Tip: To make it even healthier, use skinned chicken legs in this menu; it will still be wonderful.

NOTES ON THE MENU
Couscous with Dates and Carrots (page 84) makes an interesting alternative to rice in this menu. Dried apricots and toasted almonds—along with the grapes—make a quick, no-fuss dessert.

EGGPLANT DIP
WITH TOASTED PITA BREAD

Makes about 3 cups

I don't know why, but eggplant baked in the oven takes on a wonderful smoky flavor, here enhanced by garlic and sesame paste. The dip has a pleasingly smooth texture, too, since the eggplant is cooked until it is quite soft.

2 medium eggplants (about
   2 pounds)
1 large clove garlic, quartered
2 tablespoons tahini (sesame paste)
2 tablespoons mayonnaise
1 tablespoon fresh lemon juice

½ teaspoon salt
3 plum tomatoes, cored and finely
   chopped (about ½ pound)
Fresh pepper
4 or more medium pita breads

1. Preheat the oven to 400°. Pierce the eggplants several times with a knife. Place them on a baking sheet and bake for 35–45 minutes, or until a knife goes in easily but the flesh is still slightly firm.

2. When the eggplants are cool enough to handle, peel off the skin, using a sharp knife to help if necessary. Discard the skin. In a food processor, purée the eggplant and all the remaining ingredients except the tomatoes, pepper and pita. Turn out into a bowl, stir in the tomatoes and season with pepper and more salt, if needed.

Cut each pita bread in 6 wedges, crisp them in the oven and serve with the dip.

Party Pantry: Stocking Up for Unexpected Guests

This list will help you keep the larder stocked with foods you can serve from the can, jar or package with little or no dressing up, for quick snacks.

- Nuts, popcorn, potato chips, corn chips
- Dried and glacé fruits; jars of fancy preserved fruit
- Assorted crackers and cocktail biscuits
- Canned ham, chicken, pâté, smoked turkey
- Anchovies, sardines, olive oil-packed tuna
- Smoked mussels and oysters

- Taramasalata
- Marinated mushrooms, artichoke hearts
- Roasted peppers, pickled peppers
- Caponata
- Sun-dried tomatoes, olives, pickles
- Imported cookies, macaroons, shortbread
- Chocolates, mints and other candies

MIDDLE EASTERN YOGURT-BAKED CHICKEN LEGS

Makes plenty for 6

Tender, lemony and tangy, with no yogurt taste (strange, but often true of cooked yogurt dishes). The chicken is absolutely great the second day, if you have leftovers.

Start marinating the chicken in the morning or on the day before you want to serve it. Don't cheat on this step—it makes all the difference, because the chicken will be thoroughly permeated with the marinade.

9–11 whole chicken legs (thigh and drumstick), skinned if desired
3 cups plain (unflavored) yogurt
6 medium plum tomatoes, cored and diced (about 1 pound)

¾ cup chopped onion (about 1 medium)
1 cup (packed) flat-leaf (Italian) parsley leaves, chopped
1 teaspoon salt

1. Pierce each chicken leg 6 or 7 times with a sharp kitchen fork.

In a large bowl, stir together the remaining ingredients to make a marinade. Add the chicken and stir to coat thoroughly. With the chicken well submerged in the marinade, cover the bowl and leave it in the refrigerator all day or overnight.

2. When you are ready to cook the chicken, arrange the marinated legs in a single layer in a shallow baking dish with all the marinade. Bring to room temperature while you preheat the oven

to 375° (350° for a glass dish). Bake, uncovered, for 1½ hours, basting several times, until the chicken is very tender. The yogurt will separate, but don't be concerned about it.

Transfer the chicken to a platter, cover lightly with foil and keep warm in a low oven.

3. Pour everything else—liquid, curds, tomatoes, etc.—into a saucepan and simmer briskly until there is almost no liquid left, about 20 minutes. Spoon the sauce over the chicken and serve hot.

CUCUMBER, CHICK PEA AND RED ONION SALAD

Makes about 4½ cups

Make this salad as soon as you put the Middle Eastern chicken in the oven to bake; by the time the chicken is done and the sauce is ready, the salad will be properly marinated and ready to serve, too.

3 cucumbers, trimmed and peeled
1 medium red onion, sliced as thin
   as possible
Salt
½ cup cider vinegar
2 tablespoons sugar

1 tablespoon minced fresh dill
Fresh pepper
1¾–2 cups canned chick peas,
   rinsed and drained (one 1-pound
   can)

1. Cut the cucumbers in half lengthwise and scoop out the seeds. Slice very thin. Put the cucumbers and onions in a colander, sprinkle liberally with salt and toss well. Let them drain in the colander for 30 minutes, then rinse well and drain again.

2. In a large bowl, stir together the vinegar, sugar, dill and a good grinding of pepper. Add the cucumbers, onions and chick peas and mix well. Allow to marinate in the refrigerator for at least 1 hour, stirring occasionally. Serve chilled.

 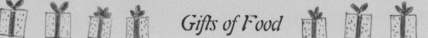

Gifts of Food

Any time of year, on any occasion, food is a universally appropriate gift. Whether it's chocolate Santas for the kids' Christmas or elegant cocktail tidbits for grown-up birthdays, edible gifts are always received with pleasure. Here are some gift-giving (and gift-wrapping) suggestions:

• **Picnic Special:** canned ham, French bread, mustard, jar of cornichons and a split of champagne tucked into a small knapsack or bookbag

• **Sweet-Tooth Treats:** an old-style cookie tin packed with nut brittle, dried peaches and pears, imported chocolate bars and a jar of butterscotch or chocolate sauce

• **Kid's Giant Birthday Cookie:** an 8- or 9-inch-diameter homemade chocolate chip cookie decorated with colored frosting and the name of the birthday child

• **Good Morning Basket:** a pretty basket lined with a checked napkin, filled with packets of tea, coffee beans, an unusual pancake or muffin mix, wild honey

WALNUT-HONEY CAKE

Makes 1 square one-layer cake

This is not, as you might expect in this menu, a typical Middle Eastern flaky pastry drowning in honey and chopped nuts. On the contrary, it's a moist, walnut-studded cake with a light topping of honey and butter. Coffee is the secret ingredient.

For the cake
1 cup coarsely chopped walnuts
1¾ cups flour
Scant teaspoon baking powder
Scant teaspoon baking soda
¼ teaspoon salt
Scant teaspoon cinnamon
⅛ teaspoon ground nutmeg
2 eggs

⅓ cup (packed) dark brown sugar
2½ tablespoons margarine or
    butter, melted and cooled
⅔ cup honey
⅓ cup cold strong coffee

For the topping
2½ tablespoons butter
2½ tablespoons honey

1. Preheat the oven to 350°; grease and flour a 9-inch square baking pan.

Toss the walnuts with 1 tablespoon of the flour; set aside. Whisk together the remaining flour, the baking powder, baking soda, salt and spices. Set aside.

2. In a large bowl, beat the eggs and brown sugar only until blended. Add the margarine or butter and honey and beat again.

3. Add the coffee and dry ingredients alternately, in 3 parts each, beating just until smooth after each addition. Stir in the nuts. Pour the batter into the prepared pan.

4. Bake for 50–60 minutes, or until a cake tester inserted in the center of the cake comes out clean.

5. While the cake is baking, prepare the topping by melting the butter and honey together.

When the cake is done and while it is still hot and in the pan, pour on the warm honey-butter mixture and brush it evenly over the top. Return the cake to the oven for 2 minutes, until the topping is absorbed. Let the cake cool in the pan on a wire rack for 10 minutes, then turn out carefully to finish cooling, right side up, on the rack.

Cut in squares and serve alone or with slightly sweetened whipped cream if you like.

INDEX